MW01093312

Totus Tuus:

Totally Yours

33 Days to Marian Consecration for Teens

Mark and Katie Hartfiel

Copyright © 2018 Hearts United, Inc.

All rights reserved.

ISBN-13: 978-1981713172
ISBN-10: 1981713174

Cover art: Lisa Mammina, The Elegant Stylist
Cover photography: Gigi Sanders photography, www.gigisanders.com

ACKNOWLEDGMENTS

Thank you Blessed Mother for calling us to your Son through your intercession. You have changed our lives and marriage. Thank you also to the Militia Mariae, who have walked this journey to Jesus with us so many times over the years. In particular, thank you to Shannon Dowlearn and Rachel Cantrell for your invaluable assistance with edits and content. To all who will help spread this book, thank you for joining in the mission and message- our prayers are with you!

DEDICATION

To the Militia Mariae

CONTENTS

Daily Consecration Prayer

Jesus, you are the Lord, King of Universe and King of my Heart. Thank you for the gift of your Mother! Jesus, I have failed you so many times. You are so good to me in that you don't give me what I deserve. I desire to take Mary into my heart and my home.

Mary, tabernacle of Christ, bring your Son to me. You are virtuous, beautiful, humble, sinless, Immaculate, my Mother and my example. I am confident in you! I choose you, Mary, to carry me to Christ. I hold nothing back. I consecrate myself to you for the glory of God. Mary, I received Christ through you and I pray he will receive me in the same way. I want all that he has for me.

Totus Tuus! I am totally yours.

Amen

Forward

To say that the Hartfiels changed my life, might be a bit of an oversell; but the Marian Consecration certainly changed my life, and they were the ones who told me about it!

I remember it like it was yesterday. As we walked out of Mass into a beautiful May morning, Mark said, "Have you ever consecrated yourself to Our Lady?" I hadn't. I had never even heard of that. I barely prayed the Rosary. Truth be known, I had for many years been stuck with a rather Protestant mentality towards Mary.

Mark nonchalantly explained the consecration, saying that it was from St. Louis de Montfort and highly recommended by Pope John Paul II (my hero, who had just died a month before). I thanked him for the thought in the sort of way one thanks grandma for that ugly sweater you are never going to wear and headed home.

I don't know what prayer Mark and Katie prayed for me as they went home, but as I rode home on my motorcycle, I could not shake the invitation. I remember thinking something like this, "All the saints unanimously recommend a close relationship with Mary. If they are wrong, then they were wrongly canonized, and the Church is a fraud, in which case, I should stop being Catholic. Or they are right, in which case, I should do it..." I started the very next day, and 33 days later I consecrated myself to Jesus through Mary on the Feast of the Immaculate Heart of Mary in the same church where I had been baptized 24 years before—and my life has never been the same!

Important to note is that I did not do the consecration because of an overwhelming filial affection for the Blessed Virgin. Nor did I do it motivated by a profound theological understanding of her role as Co-Redemptrix or Medatrix of All Graces. I did it because of the Hartfiels, JPII, and the Saints. I did it because I was Catholic and wanted to remain Catholic. But after I did it, that is when I fell in love with her!

When you open the door of your heart to Mary—even just a tiny crack—she moves right in and makes herself at home. All you have to do is give her permission, and she will do the rest. As I ponder these past 12 years, I can see her influence in every facet of my life and vocation. My faith is stronger today than it ever was. My love for Jesus today is more pure than ever before. My fidelity to the Church and commitment to my priestly vocation grows every day. My only regret is that I didn't take Mama Mary's hand when I was even younger. That the Hartfiels are making this devotion available to the youth is a great gift to the Church. I am confident that it will change many lives!

-Fr. Kyle Kowalczyk, Archdiocese of Saint Paul and Minneapolis

Introduction

Several years ago, we worked in youth ministry at a large parish in Houston, Texas. After being exposed to Marian Consecration in college and seeing its profound impact on our lives, we were compelled to teach this practice to the teens we worked with. We wrote the first draft of this book in 2006 and began to use it annually with our leadership team, affectionately called, "Militia Mariae," Latin for "Mary's Army." Our teens would meet during lunch at school for daily prayer and consecration preparation. At the same time, we also consecrated our parish's entire Life Teen program to Mary, asking her to do with it what she willed. We would definitely mark the beginning of this practice as a pivotal turning point for our teens and youth ministry program. Hearts were set on fire; lives were changed. With no doubt, Mary keeps her promises.

Now, many years later, we feel called to see if this message will find practice outside of our parish. Once again, we hope to let the Blessed Mother decide how far it can go. As the idea to publish this book was laid on our hearts, unsolicited confirmations started pouring in. Within a few months, we visited with Shannon and Grayson, who were dating as high school seniors when they consecrated themselves with us… only to renew their consecration during their wedding six years later. About a month later, during lunch with a girl named Katie, she shared the news that she was entering a Marian religious order as a result of her devotion that began with her consecration in High School. Next was a random text from FOCUS missionary, Rachel, who explained that her 33-day journey was what taught her how to really pray. About a week later, while speaking at an out-of-state conference, we ran into a former teen of ours turned seminarian, Kyle, who suddenly brought up his Marian Consecration as a defining moment in his faith. Just as any meddling mother wants to help their child find true joy, fulfillment and peace in their lives and vocation, Mary wants to guide you to yours. We are willing to promise that if you say yes to her, she will say yes to you.

You see, you couldn't have picked up this book unless the Lord had first chosen you. By agreeing to start this journey, you've already begun to imitate Mary in her "yes" to God's call. Let us join with teens across the country, faithful across the world, Saints across the ages and the Blessed Mother herself as she beckons you close to the heart of her Son. We take our first step on this journey at Calvary, with these words:

Consecrating the World to the Immaculate Heart of Mary means drawing near, through the Mother's intercession, to the very fountain of life that sprang from Golgatha. This Fountain pours forth unceasingly redemption and grace… It is a ceaseless source of new life and holiness. Consecrating the world to the Immaculate Heart of the Mother means returning beneath the Cross of the Son. It means consecrating this world to the Pierced Heart of the Savior, bringing it back to the very source of its redemption.

- Pope John Paul II, Fatima, May 13, 1982- One year after he was shot

Dear Jesus, we are here for you… let us begin.

Why Marian Consecration?

When we were expecting our second daughter, our oldest child, Maria, was ecstatic about welcoming a sister into the world. Toward the end of the pregnancy, we heard of a friend who was also expecting a baby girl but was surprised by a boy on delivery day! Hormonal and overly anxious, the decision was made to mentally prepare our three-year-old just in case the same thing happened to us. Nervousness took over as we sat her down and asked, "Maria, what would happen if we got to the hospital and when the baby was born the doctor said, 'Uh-oh, we were wrong! It's a baby boy!'" Stone-faced, she turned to us and said, "Could that happen?" In a frantic effort to smooth the rising tension, we explained, "It would be okay, right? We would love him the same! We would just have to buy some boy toys and boy clothes. We would be fine though, don't you think?" Maria shrugged and simply said, "Okay." Relief swept over us the hypothetical scenario seemed to be less intimidating than before. A few moments passed and Maria spoke up. "Mommy, what would happen if we got to the hospital and when the baby was born the doctor said, 'Uh-oh, we were wrong! It's a baby grandma!'"

Clearly, we would've had much bigger problems than boy toys and boy clothes in this situation. Thankfully, the baby came and there were no surprise boys or senior citizens! As we discussed this hilarious exchange as a couple, we found it mind-blowing that the person existing within me was essentially a stranger. The fact that children develop within their mother is widely accepted yet rarely questioned— that is, until it happens to you. Experiencing such growth of life is quite bizarre! A human person that we had never met (who could've turned out to be a boy, girl or grandma, for all we knew) was alive inside my body! Even more, this person, with her heartbeat and eternal soul, existed for weeks before we even knew she existed! No one felt any different and it didn't immediately affect our daily life or the choices we made. Yet, that didn't make this life within me any less true.

Infinitely more astonishing is that by the virtue of your Baptism, the God of the Universe, full of immeasurable power and glory, has chosen **your heart** for his dwelling place. Whether you know it or feel it and regardless of how it changes your decisions or daily life, you can't make his life within you any less true.

The purpose of this book is to draw attention to that very presence within you. What would life be like if we were constantly aware of the Lord breathing into our conversations, choices, relationships and hearts? What difference would it make in our lives? We strongly believe it would change *everything*. Each second would have rich meaning, every minute would contain complete joy and every day would be lived abundantly.

The goal of this book is quite simple. Who better to guide us on this path of discovering Jesus alive in us than the woman who lived this both spiritually and physically? If you are looking for God's presence in your life, look no further. The Blessed Virgin Mary knows just where to find him.

There is so much to say about Mary, (and you can find more about Marian Devotion in the Appendix starting on page 135) but the crux of this type of Consecration is a surrender to an intimate plan that God has in store for you today.

However, if you're like us, you know this is hard. Maybe you have romanticized how easy it must have been to have a strong faith during the Biblical times. You may ask what was it like to encounter the Lord when he was moving so freely, loudly and publicly among mankind? Many years have passed since then... thousands in fact. Approximately 3800 years ago, God spoke to the prophet Abraham. 3300 years ago, Moses led God's people from Egypt, and 3000 years ago King David founded Jerusalem. It's been 2600 years since the Temple was destroyed, and 2200 since Judas Maccabees helped Israel gain independence. Of course, 2000 years ago, Jesus the Christ is born. Roughly 100 years later, the last book of the New Testament was written.

Throughout human history, it seemed that God made a habit of working in a way that penetrated the daily life and the hearts of the human race— and he did so every few generations. Yet, the age of the Scriptures ended quite some time ago. It is easy to look at our world and question: *what has God been doing for the last 1900 years?*

Yet, what if we proposed that you live in the most spiritually significant age in human history, with the exception of the Incarnation of Christ? The epic battle between good and evil is being played out before our very eyes and God has not gone silent. On the contrary, he has been sending his most trusted disciple to speak directly to his faithful. The new question becomes, *do we have the eyes of faith to see and courage to listen?*

For the last several hundred years, the Blessed Mother has been appearing regularly and boldly in locations scattered around the world. From Wisconsin to Portugal, Mexico to France and many locations in between, the Blessed Mother has come with the same message: a universal call for us to run to Jesus—and to allow her to run alongside us.

At the dawn of this period that many theologians have dubbed "The Age of Mary," the Blessed Mother appeared to a young nun in Paris, France. As she stood before St. Catherine Laboure, rays of light extended from her hands and fell on the earth. Of course, we now know this image to be the picture imprinted on the Miraculous Medal. As St. Catherine knelt in prayer with Mary, she noticed that only some of these rays were reaching the world below. Others fell short of reaching the globe. When Catherine questioned her about these shortened rays, Mary replied, "Those are the graces for which people forget to ask."

If you're done with mediocrity, prepared to dive deep, up for an epic journey of superabundant blessings and ready to ask for those forgotten graces pouring out upon the earth then this book is for you! The Blessed Virgin Mary has come with a message for the faithful and she is repeating it with increasing urgency and passion each passing day. The Lord didn't create you to live in the Biblical times of old, but he did create you to exist **right now**. The Lord of the Universe could have placed you at any moment in his story – but here you are, in the Age of Mary. This isn't a coincidence, and we invite you to find out why…

Using This Book

If you're a teen, you're probably stressed out. We are always looking for short-cuts, efficiency and ways to make life easier. St. Louis De Montefort calls Marian Consecration the "safest, easiest, shortest and most perfect way of approaching Jesus."[1] In my life, I need the shortest, quickest, simplest way to do everything. When I first heard this phrase in regards to holiness, my heart screamed, "Sign me up!"

The word *consecrate* means "to set aside for something holy." An act of consecration means that we devote ourselves fully to the Lord, asking that he become a part of every love, struggle, victory and decision of our lives. This conscience decision of consecration will keep faith from being another extracurricular activity and, instead, let our relationship with the Lord be the center of our lives.

An Act of Consecration to Jesus through Mary is exactly what it says it is. By setting ourselves aside as Mary's, she will cultivate our hearts and deliver us directly to her Son. In the following pages, you will discover the beauty and simplicity of this pathway to holiness. Like any good mother, Mary will support, guide and intercede for you as she points you in the only direction she can: to Jesus.

In order to prepare for your Act of Consecration, it will take 33

---

[1] True Devotion to Mary Paragraph 55

days of training. In the pages that follow, we will look to the Scriptures to guide us as we dive into the Good News about the Lord, his creation, his Mother and his plan for our lives. The next 33 days won't be the consecration itself but rather a preparation for the big day. It will strengthen your spiritual muscles, which will be both challenging and incredibly rewarding. After the 33rd day, you will pray an Act of Consecration, making your commitment in a unique and powerful way. Thankfully, you won't have to walk alone. You will have the expert, who will reveal the shortest, quickest and most proficient way to reach your goal. Mary will be your trainer to help ensure that every prayer, reflection and examination is done in the most refined way possible. Just as even the best Olympian has a coach to help tweak and perfect their skill, we will have the Blessed Mother mold us for 33 days to prepare for the moment of a lifetime!

The book in your hands presents your preparation and consecration in an approachable and easy way. Loosely based on the model of St. Louis De Montefort, we will examine five areas of our spiritual life through Scripture, prayer and reflection. These are:

1. The Good News: Days 1 – 4
2. Transformation in Christ: Days 5 – 9
3. Awareness of Self: Days 10 – 17
4. Our Lady: Days 18 – 28
5. Our Lord: Days 29 – 33

Each day will contain the same format:

1. Begin with a Scripture passage. Grab your Bible and take some time to slowly read, process, and absorb the verse.
2. Next, you'll find a short reflection and some words from the Saints to help bring this passage into your own life.

3. Lastly, you'll flip to the end of each section to find the specific prayers for each section.

This 33-day journey and the Act of Consecration that completes it can be done at any time. However, some people enjoy ending on a Marian Feast Day to celebrate their consecration day. If you'd like, you can use the following chart to determine when to begin and end your 33-day preparation for Consecration to Jesus through Mary.

Day One	Consecration Day	Feast Day
January 9	February 11	Our Lady of Lourdes
February 20	March 25	Annunciation
April 10	May 13	Our Lady of Fatima
April 19	May 24	Mary Help of Christians
April 28	May 31	Visitation
Different Each Year	June	Immaculate Heart of Mary
May 25	June 27	Our Lady of Perpetual Help
June 13	July 16	Our Lady of Mount Carmel
July 13	August 15	Assumption
July 20	August 22	Queenship of Mary
August 6	September 8	Nativity of Mary

August 10	September 12	Holy Name of Mary
August 13	September 15	Our Lady of Sorrows
September 4	October 7	Our Lady of Rosary
October 17	November 19	Our Lady of Divine Providence
October 19	November 21	Presentation of Mary
October 25	November 27	Our Lady of the Miraculous Medal
November 5	December 8	Immaculate Conception
November 9	December 12	Our Lady of Guadalupe
November 29	January 1	Mary Mother of God
December 31	February 2	Our Lady of Good Success

Divine Slavery and "Totus Tuus"

───────○(つ◡ᗑC)○───────

In his book, *True Devotion to Mary*, St. Louis De Montefort expresses his desire to consecrate himself fully to Jesus through Mary by saying, "Totus tuus ego sum, et omnia mea tua sunt. Accipio te in mea omnia. Praebe mihi cor tuum, Maria." This translates, "I belong entirely to you, and all that I have is yours. I take you for my all. O Mary, give me your heart."[2] This phrase, "Totus Tuus," became St. John Paul II's motto for his papacy. Could anyone ever think of a more perfect and deserving motto for our own lives? Totus Tuus— or "Totally Yours" sums up everything we want to be. We want to empty ourselves of all that we are and belong completely to Jesus through Mary. As Pope Benedict XVI said, "Do not be afraid of Christ, he takes nothing away and gives you everything." We don't have to be afraid to give the Blessed Mother every fiber of our mind, heart and body, knowing that she will make sure all of our holy desires exceed anything we could imagine. *Totus Tuus Maria*, we want to be totally yours!

Upon completion of the 33-day journey and Act of Consecration, many people choose give themselves a gift as a reminder of their gift to Mary. Of course, we Catholics love physical

---

[2] Saint Louis de Montfort, Treatise on True Devotion to the Blessed Virgin, 266

reminders of spiritual realities. A suggested symbol of this commitment is the practice of wearing a chain signifying your connection to the Blessed Mother. St. Louis de Montfort used the image of "holy slavery" to describe how closely he wanted to follow Mary's example. He decided to wear chains on his arms and feet as a token of his love for her. He strongly recommended, after his own example (and that of many other saints), that those who consecrate themselves to Mary also wear a chain around their wrist or ankle.

St. Louis De Montefort explains that in this world we find ourselves chained to the devil through our sins. If you're like us, you find yourself repeating the same sins time and time again in the confessional. This proves that we aren't free but bound to the choices we make. Holy slavery is a decision to ask the Blessed Mother to work ardently with us, to break the chains of sin and death in our lives and to do so by drawing close to her mothering arms. As St. Louis De Montefort describes in his own words:

Thus set free, we are bound to Jesus and Mary not by compulsion and force like galley-slaves, but by charity and love as children are to their parents. "I shall draw them to me by chains of love" said God Most High speaking through the prophet. Consequently, these chains are as strong as death, and in a way stronger than death, for those who wear them faithfully till the end of their life. For though death destroys and corrupts their body, it will not destroy the chains of their slavery, since these, being of metal, will not easily corrupt. It may be that on the day of their resurrection, that momentous day of final judgment, these chains, still clinging to their bones, will contribute to their glorification and be transformed into chains of light and splendour. Happy then, a thousand times happy, are the illustrious slaves of Jesus in Mary who bear their chains even to the grave.[3]

---

[3] Ibid, 237

Of course, this practice is completely optional. If you do decide to wear a chain, there are several possibilities of how you can do so. Most people head to the hardware store and purchase a small bit of chain to attach to their wrist. Some even attach it in a way that it cannot be removed, while others add a small clasp. There is something extremely gratifying about watching the metal change colors with age as your devotion to Mary also marinates over the years. Others opt to buy a higher quality chain bracelet or necklace and attach a Marian medal to it. No matter what you decide, a dash of Holy Water or priestly blessing will make any choice a good one.

Introduction to

Days 1-4

The Good News

Newsflash… Breaking news… Newsfeeds…
Sound bites… 280 Characters… Abbrevs…

If there is one thing the youth of the 21st Century have, it's news. What makes news good news per se? What makes news life-altering? What news can reach to the depth of your heart, into the corners no one else has seen – and change everything?

Only the news that is also a person could accomplish such a thing. Jesus himself is the Word (Jn 1:1). Scripture further explains that "Indeed, the word of God is living and effective, sharper than any two-edged sword, penetrating even between soul and spirit, joints and marrow and able to discern reflections and thoughts of the heart" (Heb 4:12). The Good News is found in God's Word, and it is here that we encounter a person… a person who is seeking YOU.

Just over 2000 years ago, God literally took on the flesh of humanity. He became one of us so that we could be one with him. He was born, grew, learned, walked, slept, ate, prayed and wept. He lived the life of a human and sacrificed himself for us even unto death on a cross.

Jesus is our only way back to God the Father. He is the only bridge that gaps the infinite distance between man and God. He is the only one who can save us from sin and death. He is the only one who can take our place and nail our sins to the cross. He is the only one who can bring good out of evil. He is the only one who can give us abundant life. Finally, and most importantly, he is the only one who can bring us home to the Father. This isn't just Good News… it is THE News that changes everything.

Day 1

Good News: You are The Now of the Church

Grab your Bible and let the words from
St. Paul to Timothy sink in:

Daily Reading: 1 Timothy 4:12

We all want to do great things in our lives. Even as children, we are encouraged to set goals and have high aspirations. Yet, it seems like the day for true greatness is forever in the future. It is simple and exciting to say "someday" and intimidating to say "now."

The book of Jeremiah is one of the most widely recognized books in the Old Testament. In the first chapter, God gets straight to the point as he addresses Jeremiah. God tells him, "I have appointed you to be a prophet to the nations" (Jer. 1:5). Imagine that in this moment, the Lord speaks and informs you that you will be an instrument to change history. What if he said you will do great things in his name and thousands of years later people will read your story and encounter God through it? How would you respond?

Jeremiah's reply in this situation is neither surprising nor inspiring, but it does speak to the authenticity of the Scriptures. Jeremiah actually tries to change God's mind! In his confusion, Jeremiah wonders why God would choose him. He explains that he is simply too young for such a task. God, in his wisdom, confidently answers Jeremiah, "Say not 'I am too young' to whomever I send you, you shall go; whatever I command you, you shall speak. Have

26

no fear before them, because I am with you to deliver you..."" (Jer. 1:7).

God didn't choose an elder, a priest, a famous political leader or a great speaker. He chose Jeremiah – a man who was not only young, but the perfect candidate for the job. Let the words of St. Paul in today's reading from the book of Timothy speak straight and *personally* to your heart.

Saint John Paul II knew the power of young people when he said, "The youth are not the future of the Church, they are the *now*." This message doesn't refer to just Timothy or Jeremiah, it's about you. You can truly can set the example and be a light to the nations in "speech, conduct, love, faith and purity." The Lord is calling, how will you respond?

Christ has confidence in young people and entrusts them with the very future of his mission, "Go and make disciples". Go beyond the confines of what is humanly possible and create a world of brothers and sisters!
– Pope Francis

Prayers for Days 1-4 located on page 34

Day 2

The Good News: He Paid Our Debt

Daily Reading: Romans 8:1-2, 31-39

Our one year old daughter, Lucy, recently learned to walk. To be honest, she was pretty awful at it at first. She would make it only a step or two before she fell. However, no one was surprised or disappointed – including Lucy. This was expected and over time, with encouragement and practice, she improved. Soon she will master this skill and move on to new challenges that will be difficult initially but will soon become natural.

Both on this pathway to Consecration and on your Christian journey, you may get discouraged with yourself at times. You will fall. You will sin. You will fail to be perfect. There may even be a certain offense that you feel you can never overcome. There will undoubtedly be times when you feel unworthy and have the temptation of despair.

The mystery of God's love is that it does not matter what you have done deep in the past, how you messed up yesterday or what you did two minutes ago. We can fall a million times over, but if we seek Christ through the Sacrament of Reconciliation, there is no condemnation. He has freed us from our sins and washed them in his blood. He has paid our debts – even those hidden in the most secret places of our heart! We are free and we are forgiven. Christ died and rose from every sin ever committed— no sin is too great. If you are struggling, then he came precisely for YOU. He didn't come for the righteous, but for the sinners (Lk 5:32, Mk 2:17, Mt 9:13).

Christ meets all of us **exactly** where we are and takes us further. Many feel that they need to be perfect in order to approach Christ. Imagine you come home from practice covered in sweat and mud. Do you have to clean up before you take a shower? Of course not! Jesus is the way to be truly clean and truly free. Go to Him! Christ wants us to come as we are – sin and all. He longs to shower his mercy upon us. When we are in Christ, nothing can separate us from his love.

Resolve today to never despair. Even when you fall, run to his mercy no matter how many times it takes. The Good News is that Christ is Mercy himself and that he never grows weary of forgiving us. Go forth in freedom!

"God's greatest pleasure is to pardon us."
-St. John Vianney

Prayers for Days 1-4 located on page 34

Day 3

The Good News: Your Call to an Abundant Life

Daily Reading: John 10:7-11

What does it mean to "live life to the full?" Let's hope that it's more than YOLO and other "epic" hashtags. Ask yourself, do I experience abundant life? Do I even know what an abundant and full life looks like? Jesus became man precisely to show us. He promised us this life if we decide to give our lives to him.

Every human person is seeking happiness. We are constantly yearning and longing for something to fill us. Humanity seeks to quench this thirst with all sorts of pleasures that the world has to offer: sex, food, money, power, fame and success. The world advertises these things to us extensively, without ever letting us up for air. We can say that we aren't fooled, yet we analyze our peer's opinions, obsessively check social media and hunger to be desired. However, when we indulge in these things, the satisfaction is counterfeit and quickly passing. It is not surprising that we live in a world where so many people are bored and depressed.

This is not what Jesus had in mind in today's passage from John. God wants to shatter our expectations of what a "full life" looks like. Unlike our tendency, God doesn't just do the minimum – he is a God of superabundant excess. Just look out the window and see that we don't have one tree, but millions. We don't have one lake with the exact amount of water the world needs, but oceans that are so deep that no man-made machine can explore the depths. We don't have just one star, but billions of galaxies. God's limitlessness is written everywhere. This is God's plan for your abundant life – to pour put this same sort of excess of love, mercy and grace into you.

Jesus wants to give you something that can't be taken away. This is why the early Christians could walk to their death singing; they knew that their God wasn't limited even by the grave. Wouldn't you love that freedom? If the threat of execution couldn't shake your trust in this Good Shepherd, then no amount of drama could do so either. Jesus doesn't promise an easy life but rather an abundant one. All you have to do is take him up on his offer.

"Do not be afraid of Christ! He takes nothing away, and he gives you everything. When we give ourselves to him, we receive a hundredfold in return. Yes, open, open wide the doors to Christ – and you will find true life." - Pope Benedict XVI

Prayers for Days 1-4 located on page 34

31

Day 4

The Good News: Christ's Victory over The Struggle

Daily Reading: Romans 7:13-25

Today's reading can be summed up in four words: story.of.my.life. This is exactly the sentiment I feel standing in the confession line asking myself, "Why did I think that was a good idea?" St. Paul relates, "I do not do what I want, but I do what I hate... I do not do the good I want, but I do the evil I do not want." We were created to desire Heaven, yet we condemn ourselves and choose against it time and time again. Why do we fall from the resolution to avoid sin? We long for what is true, good and fulfilling and yet choose counterfeit, destruction and emptiness. We are stressed and torn through a spiritual tug-of-war.

St. Paul recognizes the conflict between the good he hungers for and the sin that almost seems to puppeteer his actions. The choice is ours, but the pull can be so strong. When Adam and Eve were tempted, Satan twisted the truth to make sin appear good and attractive. Consequently, we became a people who starve for goodness but are fatally attracted to sin. Our own modern temptations are equally as appealing as the fruit from the tree, and we repeatedly fall prey to the lies. We are left feeling guilty in the aftermath, wondering why we do not do what we want but do what we hate.

St. Paul asks desperately at this end of this passage, "who will deliver me?" St. Paul understood that if left to himself, he would continue to be under the power of sin. Left to ourselves, the devil will trick us every time. Even if we long to do well in our hearts, our minds are easily won over. Satan is intellectually superior to us, and, if we get into a dialogue with him, we will surely lose.

Christ is our only answer! It is only in "putting on the mind of Christ" that we will triumph over sin. By allowing Christ to fight your battles, nothing can stand in your way. In times of temptation, let Jesus renew your mind and claim his victory (Rom. 12:2). Give these tempting moments to the Lord in prayer and fasting. Find Jesus in a friend through accountability. Most of all encounter him often in the Sacraments. He wants your freedom even more than you do. Believe it.

"Apart from the Cross, there is no other ladder by which we may get to heaven." - St. Rose of Lima

Prayers for Days 1-4 located on page 34

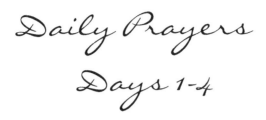

Daily Prayers
Days 1-4

Our Father

Our Father, Who art in heaven, hallowed be thy name. Thy Kingdom come. Thy will be done, on earth as it is in Heaven. Give us this day our daily bread and forgive us our trespasses, as we forgive those who trespass against us. Lead us not into temptation, but deliver us from evil. Amen.

Hail Mary

Hail Mary, Full of grace, the Lord is with you. Blessed are you among women and blessed is the fruit of your womb, Jesus. Holy Mary, Mother of God, pray for us sinners, now and at the hour of our death. Amen.

Glory Be

Glory Be to the Father, the Son and the Holy Spirit. As it was in the beginning is now and ever shall be, world without end. Amen

Prayer to the Holy Spirit

Come Holy Spirit, fill the hearts of the faithful and enkindle in them the fire of your love. Send forth your Spirit, and they shall be created, and you shall renew the face of the earth. Amen

Prayer to Saint Michael

Saint Michael, the Archangel, defend us in battle. Be our protection against the wickedness and snares of the Devil. May God rebuke him we humbly pray, and do thou, O prince of the Heavenly Host, by the power of God, cast into hell, Satan and all the evil spirits who prowl about the world seeking the ruin of souls. Amen

Prayer to Guardian Angel

Angel of God, my Guardian Dear, to whom God's love commits me here. Ever this day/night be at my side, to light and guard, to rule and guide. Amen

Act of Contrition

Oh my God, I am heartfully sorry for having offended thee. I detest all of my sins because of your most just punishment, but mostly because I have offended you whom I should love above all things. I firmly resolve with the help of thy grace to sin no more and to avoid the near occasion of sin. Amen

Closing Prayer

Jesus, I love you. Give me the desire to desire you.
I place myself in your presence.
Help me to know that you are dwelling within me always. Amen

Spend a few moments in silence.

"The Lord tells us: 'the first task in life is this: prayer.' But not the prayer of words, like a parrot; but the prayer of the heart: gazing on the Lord, hearing the Lord, asking the Lord." – Pope Francis

Introduction to Days 5-9

Transformation in Christ

When we become comfortable in our faith, we know it's time to move forward. Jesus Christ loves us right where we are, but he loves us too much to leave us there. Jesus knows our full potential, and he longs for us grow into the individuals he created us to be! You can't have a testimony without a test, and our transformation in Christ is a story that is continually being written. In these next five days, we will be challenged to transform. To grow in an authentic Christian life, we must always be ready for the next adventure of growth.

You were created to bask in the glory of God forever. God's happily ever after includes soaring to the heights of heaven and entering deeply into the mystery and the love of the Trinity. Amazingly, we are invited to experience a taste of this truth here and now on Earth. Lord, give us the hunger to strive for this gift without counting the cost.

Day 5

Readiness to Change

Daily Reading: Matthew 4:18-22

I would be willing to bet that one phrase in particular struck you in the gut during this reading: "They left their nets immediately and followed him." The Scriptures don't give us any indication that Simon, Andrew, James and John had a past relationship with Jesus. However, with just one sentence, they leave their old life behind in response to the invitation "Come and follow me." Why would they do this?! It's simple- an authentic encounter with the face of God is more intense than anything we could ever imagine. Their hearts "burned within them" as they recognized the voice of God calling them to be who he had designed them to be... to reach their full potential. This desire for God made it easy for these first disciples to possess a readiness to change.

In order to become a new creation in Christ, we must have an absolute disposition of willingness to change. An adventure never unfolds if the hero insists on staying safe and comfortable. We must be willing and open to becoming someone who is fundamentally different, if God wills it. This does not imply that we lose ourselves or that we become less of who we are. In fact, it is quite the opposite. *A total transformation in Christ means to become more ourselves.* We discover who we were created to be. To live true Christianity is to be fully human. The question is, do you truly want everything he has in store for you? If so, Jesus asks, will you "Come and follow me?"

"We MUST have an unconditional readiness to change in order to be transformed in Christ."
– Dietrich von Hildebrand

Prayers for Days 5-9 located on page 48

Day 6

The Call to Repent

Daily Reading: Acts 3:19-20, 8:22

"Urgency." That is what the words of the New Testament scream when they beg us to turn away from sin and fix our eyes on Jesus Christ. We don't hear Jesus say, "if you have time, turn away from sin", or "after you finish your fun, repent", or "when you are older turn to me". The overwhelming message is that the time is **now**.

Eternity has been explained as a slab of concrete a mile long and a mile thick. Imagine an ant walking from one end to the other and back again. He does this over and over again. The more times the ant completes this journey the more the concrete will begin to wear away where his tiny footprints have trod. How long do you think it would take for this ant to walk back and forth so many times that his path erodes so deep that it cuts the concrete slab in half? That amount of time is a only a fraction of a second in eternity.

How does the length of your stay on earth compare to this analogy? Our lives are less than a pinprick on the timeline of eternity. Yes, there is an urgency to turn away from sin. As our dear friend, Fr. Dave Pivonka often says, loving the Lord deeply is having knowledge that "sin isn't breaking a rule; it is breaking a heart." Sin settles like a cancer, and the longer it is ignored, the more it grows and spreads. When treated, it must be removed in its entirety to prevent its return.

Repentance means flying to the mercy of your Savior, who is aching to forgive you, especially through the gift of reconciliation. The center of repentance is rejecting future sin in your life. In the words of St. Mary Euphrasia Pelletier, "It is human to fa angelic to rise again." The first step of transformation is choosing to be more than human, which can only happen by allowing Christ's life within us.

"You cannot be half a saint. You must be a whole saint or no saint at all." -St. Therese of Lisieux

Prayers for Days 5-9 located on page 48

Day 7

The Passing World

Daily Reading: Matthew 6:9-21

It is important to note that eternal life is much more amazing than we think it is. Often times we might imagine people in white robes frolicking through lush, green grass with animals grazing by the rainbow nearby. These types of images sound like a nice vacation, but when I am in the throes of my most difficult temptations, the thought of the eternal petting zoo doesn't entice me to choose Heaven instead.

What is it that we are saved for? It is so much more! Scripture says, "What eye has not seen, and ear has not heard, and what has not entered the human heart, what God has prepared for those who love him." (1 Cor 2:9). Some describe Heaven like an unborn baby trying to imagine the world. Without references, a baby can't imagine a tree, or a mother…. not to mention that the baby doesn't even have the mental capacity to understand these concepts. Furthermore, what is the point of the womb? Naturally, you want to leave – not to stay there forever – but to be prepared and molded to be born. Have you ever wished to go back to your mother's womb? To want this would just be weird.

What is the point of earthly life? To be born into eternal life. Of course, we wouldn't cling to our time in the womb, yet when we cling to the things of the earth – it's just as crazy. When we make it to Heaven and think back to our time on earth, we won't want to return. It will so far exceed anything we can imagine. When we think of it in these terms, what else matters?

If we truly seek Heaven for what it really is, we should be able to endure all things here below. We should ask ourselves what really matters in life. All the possible worldly successes are not sufficient to get us to Heaven. What can save our souls: money, power, popularity, success or knowledge? No! All of these things are passing away.

"Earth has no sorrow that Heaven can't heal."
-St. Thomas More

Prayers for Days 5-9 located on page 48

Day 8

Heavenly Gaze

Daily Reading: Colossians 3:1-17

What is your first orientation? How do you spend most of your time? What do think about? In other words, where is your gaze? St. Paul tells us that we should fix our minds on Heaven – the things that are above!

However, countless messages bombard us every day, and the anxiety of the world easily consumes our thoughts and speech. There is no necessary reason that we should spend our lives worrying about earthly issues. Yet, how often does gossip, judgmental thoughts and negative self-reflection consume our thoughts for much of our day? We know that these worldly obsessions bring us angst, and we recognize the way we feel after media binging or gossiping but we continually come back for more.

If we fix our eyes on Christ, we find peace. When our gaze and outlook is placed in the beauty of Heaven, then the trappings of the world cannot deceive us. So many have replaced the Lord with false gods of the world, maybe without even meaning to. If we are not intentional about keeping our eyes fixed on Christ, we will be duped as well. Make a resolution to put aside the things that are listed in today's reading and instead, set your mind on things above.

Pope Francis has asked what our lives would be like if we treated our Bibles like we treat our phones. If we check it as often, looked to it for ways to solve our problems and kept it near to us always. If you make a resolution to allow your thoughts to primarily be consumed with Jesus, he will reward you by consuming you in turn.

"If men knew the meaning of eternity, they would do anything to mend their lives." - St. Jacinta of Fatima

Prayers for Days 5-9 located on page 48

Day 9

Fear Has No Power

Daily Reading: John 16:33

When choosing to give our lives to Christ and to go deeper in our spiritual lives we sometimes experience a great deal of fear and our minds toil anxiously with questions. What does Jesus want of me? What am I to do now? What does this mean for my life? What will my friends think? Will I be accepted? I am unworthy. Jesus, what do you want from me? I am afraid to abandon myself to you, Lord!

If you ever feel this way, you are not alone. When Moses came before the presence of God, he put a cover over his face (ex. 34:29-35). When Peter encountered the Lord while fishing, he proclaimed, "Depart from me Lord" (Lk 5:8). When John saw the Lord in a vision of Heaven, he fell to his face as though dead (Rev. 1:17). Why did they all react this way? The Holy Presence of God was overwhelming for them, and they were struck with a holy fear.

To each of them, Jesus spoke these consoling words, "Do not be afraid." He also spoke these very words to Abraham, Jacob, Isaiah, and Joshua. He spoke these words to the fearful apostles after he rose from the dead.

These are the words that Christ speaks to you today. "Do not be afraid." Do not be afraid to follow him. Do not fear what his plans are for your life or where he will lead you. What he has in store for you is infinitely greater than anything you could ever imagine. His ways are above your ways, and his thoughts are above your thoughts. Follow Christ with humble confidence, trusting in him for everything. Never be afraid!

"Do not be afraid." – St. John Paul II's first words as Pope.

Prayers for Days 5-9 located on page 48

Daily Prayers for Days 5-9

Our Father...
Hail Mary...
Glory Be...

Fragrance Prayer

Dear Jesus, help me to spread Your fragrance everywhere I go. Flood my soul with Your spirit and life. Penetrate and possess my whole being, so utterly, that my life may only be a radiance of Yours. Shine through me, and be so in me, that every soul I come in contact with may feel Your presence in my soul. Let them look up and see no longer me, but only Jesus! Stay with me, and then I will begin to shine as You shine; so to shine as to be a light for others. The light O Jesus will be all from You, none of it will be mine. It will be You, shining on others through me. Let me preach you without preaching, not by words but by my example, by the catching force, the sympathetic influence of what I do, the evident fullness of the love my heart bears to You. Amen.

Anima Christi

Soul of Christ, sanctify me.
Body of Christ, save me.
Blood of Christ, inebriate me.
Water from the side of Christ, wash me.
Passion of Christ, strengthen me.
O good Jesus, hear me.
Within your wounds, hide me.
Separated from you, let me never be.
From the evil one, protect me.
At the hour of my death, call me.

48

And close to you, bid me.
That with your angels and saints I may praise you forever and ever.
Amen.

"If we spent half as much time praying as we do watching TV, we would convert the whole world."
-St. Padre Pio

Introduction to
Days 10-17

Awareness of Self

During this preparation for Marian Consecration, it is important for us to recognize our status in our relationship with Jesus. Over these next several days, we will look closely at our own disposition and evaluate where we are and where we would like to be. When reaching for knowledge of self, we shouldn't focus solely on how far away we are from Jesus, but instead rely heavily on remembering that Marian Consecration is the shortest, fastest, easiest way to Jesus. But first, let's recognize that we cannot embark on this journey if we do not know our current disposition.

So far, we have heard the good news and meditated on transformation in Christ with an unconditional readiness to change. Now it is time to boldly ask the Lord over these next eight days to give you an honest assessment of yourself and a strong calling to bring you further. If we are ignorant of our defects, we will never be able to overcome them.

In a special way, we will call upon the Holy Spirit in prayer during this time. Expose yourself to the Holy Spirit, holding nothing back. Ask him to penetrate your heart and reveal your real self. Ask the Holy Spirit to enkindle your heart and mind with love, purity, passion, and a radical openness to the mercy of God. You don't have to be afraid of who you will see as the Lord reveals the depth of yourself to you. Trust the Divine Physician to not only diagnose but reveal a way of salvation. The love of the Holy Spirit will purify and sanctify us, if we open ourselves and allow him in.

Day 10

Who am I?

Daily Reading: Genesis 2:4-25

As we grow older, we become more aware of ourselves. When we are young we are basically compliant with any situation, as long as we have a handful of cheerios and no one is forcing us to go to bed too early. Yet, over time, our understanding of many things changes. We tend to be more concerned with our own self-perception and seek to discover where we fit in.

During this time of preparation for Marian Consecration, it is important to take a good look at who we are and who we were created to be. We need a foundation to stand on as we begin to propel ourselves toward our destination of drawing near to Jesus through Mary. Earnestly ask the Lord to clearly reveal the condition of your soul. Ask without fear to know what separates you from him. Desire to know the reality of the way your faults pierce his heart. Ask him to give you a hunger to change out of love for him.

It is important that this request is coupled with an earnest petition that the Lord will also show you the glory of who you are and who you were created to be. In today's reading, we should almost tremble at the excitement in God's voice as he proclaims that he has made man and woman in his own image and likeness. Truly, we bear a fingerprint of who God is because of the way he created us. St. Peter even goes so far as to say, "Through these, he has bestowed on us the precious and very great promises, so that through them you may come to *share in the divine nature*, after escaping from the corruption that is in the world because of evil desire" (2 Pet 1:4). You are a masterpiece of God, and because of that, you have an innate dignity for what God has worked in you. Let this realization compel us to fall to our knees in thanksgiving and wonder at the God of the Universe and his presence in our lives.

"God loves each one of us as though there were only one of us to be loved." St. Augustine

Prayers for Days 10-17 located on page 68

Day 11

Where Do I Stand?

Daily Reading: Luke 8:4-15

"In the beginning was the Word, and the Word was with God, and the Word was God... and the Word became flesh and made his dwelling among us" (Jn 1:1; 1:14). John's first words in his Gospel explain to his readers that the Word is Jesus Christ himself. Keeping this in mind, where do you place yourself in this parable of today's daily reading?

One thing that we can notice about each of the people listed in this story is that they all have good intentions. They desire to produce good fruit and are happy to receive the Word of God. However, most of them are unable to take root. We must remember that we have been given the gift of the Word, but with that comes action and responsibility.

Perhaps you have experienced the truth and promises of the Word of God through a retreat, camp or prayer experience. Judging by your experiences with the Word, we ask again, where do you fall into this parable? Are you the person who had joy but it was quickly removed by an attitude of apathy? Was it choked by temptation, suffering or by the situations and people you surround yourself with? Are you a person who received the Word and gift of Christ in your life and let it flourish to bring nourishment to others around you?

The secret is that we must constantly condition ourselves to accept God's Word in our lives. God can pour out every grace, blessing and opportunity on us, but if we are not willing to let it fill us, it simply won't. As an athlete prepares his body for the big event, so must we take the measures of frequenting the Sacraments, immersing ourselves in prayer and avoiding the near occasion of sin. This practice will truly create a rich soil that is ready to bring fruit to the world. What step do you need to take today to cultivate the soil of your soul?

"Give me the desire to desire you." – Unknown

Prayers for Days 10-17 located on page 68

Day 12

The Heart of the Matter

Daily Reading: John 1:35-39

Do you remember was it like being a child waiting for Christmas? As the holiday grew closer, it became harder and harder to sleep at night. It would be such a joy to bask in the magic of the day. However, within 24 hours, it was over and by the end of the week there was something new to look forward to. Whatever we do or accomplish in our lives, it always has an ending. Reaching one milestone causes us to fix our eyes on the next. Whether it is an event, a relationship or receiving a long-awaited material possession, nothing ever completely satisfies.

We, as humans, are on a constant scavenger hunt, looking for one clue that will lead to another. Our heart guides us because it is what longs to be satisfied. It is that itch that keeps us searching for more. We continually search because there is an infinite hole within us thirsting to be filled. The problem is that a bottomless hole cannot be full, even if the entire earth was placed inside.

In today's reading, Jesus asks his disciples what they are looking for and then invites them to come and see what he has to offer. Our only solution is to look to the infinite, to our God who is eternal. Jesus promises that he is the food from Heaven that will cure any desire we have. Those who come to him will cease to hunger and those who believe in him will no longer thirst. Yet, Jesus isn't speaking about our stomachs, he is speaking about our hearts.

This is the heart of the matter- it all comes down to grasping this truth. When we become a sanctuary for the eternal God, we find that we are finally fully alive. If the Lord of the Universe is an inhabitant of our hearts, we find within us a power that is greater than any power on earth.

"In the twilight of life, God will not judge us on our earthly possessions and human successes, but on how well we have loved." - St. John of the Cross

Prayers for Days 10-17 located on page 68

Day 13

New Creation

Daily Reading: Romans 6:5-11

If you're a sinner, it's important to know the difference between condemnation and conviction. Condemnation is the voice of guilt that makes us feel damaged, worthless and shameful. Conviction, on the other hand, allows us to see how we have failed and therefore *calls us to change.* This is why St. Thérèse could say that her weakness and wretchedness were like an elevator that kept her close to God. Conviction motivates us to *hold fast* to mercy.

How about you? Have you made mistakes? Have you fallen? Have you made choices you aren't proud of? Do you feel the weight of your past still on your conscience? Do you hate your sin? Welcome to the club! Even St. Paul, one of the greatest Saints, cried out to the Lord to remove the "thorn" (2 Corinthians 12:7) in his flesh- the sin he could not overcome. We may be tempted to ask why do we sin? If we have been redeemed, why do we still fall short all the time? God answers Paul and answers you "my power is made perfect in weakness." God's true nature and glory is revealed when he loves what is unlovable in us. That is amazing. His love covers our sin and our shame.

We've all heard people talk about "Catholic Guilt." The misconception is that Catholics are shamed into good behavior because of inner condemnations. On the contrary, when we make a mistake, our conscience knows we were created for more. The *healthy* version of "Catholic Guilt" gives us the drive to find out what that 'more' is all about!

The truth is that Christ has re-created us in the waters of Baptism and the mercy of Confession. Not only are we forgiven, but he makes us new! Think about how exciting it is to get a new phone. A couple of years later it is scratched, the reception and data package have slowed and it's missing all the new features... but then, the next generation arrives! Receiving this is better than refurbishing our old phone. Instead, the new one builds on the shortcomings of the first in order to become something even better. In an analogous way, through Christ's Sacramental mercy, we are "upgraded" as we go forward in his love!

Understanding who we are consists in knowing what Christ did for us. To understand who we are, we must understand that the Passion and Cross of Jesus do not simply give us a cosmetic covering of our sinfulness, but rather reconcile us children of the Father. We are made new! His mercy reaches into the depths of who we are and has the power to transform us at our core. Truly, "By his wounds, we are healed" (Is. 53:5).

"Do not go looking for [your sins] at the bottom of the sea! He has wiped them out; He has forgotten them." – St. Therese

Prayers for Days 10-17 located on page 68

Day 14

The Cost

Daily Reading: Matthew 16:24-26

I will never forget the first time our oldest child heard the story of the crucifixion. We were visiting a beautiful shrine on the East Coast, and they had these incredible statues of the Stations of the Cross set up on a path through the woods. My husband and daughter walked hand-in-hand, and I listened while he explained, age appropriately, for the first time how Jesus suffered and died. It was difficult for me to watch her little, pure self be exposed for the first time to the reality of evil in the world. But watching her wonder and awe at the magnitude of Jesus' love and seeing her acceptance of the reality of Jesus' sacrifice was indescribable.

At one point, she asked Mark why they would do something like this to Jesus. Mark was stumped. How do you explain to a four-year-old that sin is ugly, brutal and ultimately ends in death? And furthermore, how do you answer the question of "why do we sin?" The reason why this is so hard to answer is because sin doesn't make sense.

For weeks afterwards, she brought up the story of the Passion. One day when she was recounting the story, I looked right into those big brown eyes and said, "Maria, do you know what Jesus was thinking about when he went through all of that?" She clearly hadn't thought about it and looked back at me with anticipation, and asked, "What?" I replied, "He was thinking about you." Her eyes widened in disbelief and looked at me in disbelief, "Me?" she said. I went on to explain that Jesus would do anything to make sure they could be together forever.

We hear in this Gospel reading that experiencing this beautiful, intense love is a call to respond. Jesus gave every ounce of his blood to save us from the death we warranted through our decision to sin. Yet, he still promises eternal life, an act and a gift unfathomable to our human minds. Knowing the greatness of Heaven (and greatness of our God), we should be willing to pay any price to be with our Lord in Paradise.

What are the things in your life that you are not willing to lose? What are you holding on to that is a risk to your communion with God? He knows your battle because he already fought it and won. Let him walk with you as you take up your cross. Jesus promises that if you lose your life for his sake, you will find it. Relieve him of his thirst, which only *you* can satisfy.

"In the end, you will realize that it was not you who was carrying the cross, but it was the cross that was carrying you." -Father Jean C.J. d'Elbee

Prayers for Days 10-17 located on page 68

Day 15

Virtue and Vice

Daily Reading: Luke 6:43-45

Habits are an important part of our lives as human beings. It sounds elementary, but even the small parts of our day are only possible because we have learned something in the past. Walking, brushing our teeth, turning a light on, and all these things take little thought or concentration on our part because we learned to trust in our ability to complete these tasks. Even knowing our name is only possible because we learned it.

We are creatures of habit. Some of these habits, like those named above, have no direct effect on our salvation. Other habits, however, can be positive (virtues) or negative (vices). We all know that the more we practice something, the easier it becomes. This applies to our faith as well. For example, if we practice patience, although it will be hard at first, we will eventually become a patient person and act more patiently with ease and even with joy! The more virtues we have, the easier it is to master more of them. It also follows that this would be true with negative habits. If we consistently practice a vice, it will also soon become a habit. The first few times we may feel guilty about this deed, but eventually it will be done without much thought. Even our conscience begins to be silenced the more it is suppressed. Likewise, the more vices we have, the more likely we are to develop additional ones.

In order to grow in holiness and self-discipline, we must know ourselves. If we don't know which virtues we are lacking, we will not be able to try to work toward more. If we are unclear on our vices, we will not be able to conquer them. Use today's reading as an honest assessment of yourself and the type of fruit you bring forth to the world. Can people tell there is something different about you because of the habits you have formed in your life? All of us are created differently and we all have different passions and gifts. Being able to harness and direct our passions to the Lord will help launch us toward holiness. As we seek to develop a keener awareness of our passions, virtues and our vices, we can implore our Mother to guide us, just as children need earthly mothers to guide them.

"A man who governs his passions is the master of the world. We must either command them, or be enslaved by them." – St Dominic

Prayers for Days 10-17 located on page 68

Day 16

The Plank

Daily Reading: Matthew 7:1-5

Many of us spend a lot of time consumed with other people. We are made to be relational, so it makes sense that our attention and emotions gravitate toward others. While this is such an enriching and rewarding aspect of our humanity, it is also, at times, one of our biggest struggles. It is often issues involving other people that we take with us into the confessional.

In today's Scripture, we hear a verse that is both very familiar and probably very applicable to most everyone. It seems that nearly every day provides an opportunity to notice something negative about another person. These ill and judgmental thoughts and/or words are often aimed at our family, friends, enemies and sometimes even strangers! It is as if we have a radar for disapproval of others.

It is also often true that we are mesmerized by the amazing accomplishments of others. We can take, as an example, the reaction to the passing of our former Pope, St. John Paul II in 2005. For days, people of all faiths around the world were captivated by their televisions, in awe of the incredible accomplishments of this remarkable man. Surely there are people in our daily lives that we look up to with admiration and that we seek to imitate.

We shouldn't be fooled to think that we are somehow immune to the eyes of others. An old DCTalk song began with the quote, *"The greatest single cause of atheism in the world today is Christians, who proclaim Jesus with their lips and walk out the door and deny him with their lifestyle. That is what an unbelieving world simply finds unbelievable."*

We have great opportunity and responsibility to be living proclamations of the great works of Christ rather than the mere works we can accomplish on our own. With Christ as our motivation, we can authentically love others and ourselves in order to make God known in our world.

"If all men knew what others say of them, there would not be four friends in the world." -Blaise Pascal

Prayers for Days 10-17 located on page 68

Day 17

The Enemy

Daily Reading: 1 Peter 5:8-11

In 2016, we were invited to pre-screen the violent and gory war-film, *Hacksaw Ridge,* before its release. Never had we witnessed such horrific carnage, and, at times, it was impossible to watch. The film documents the true story of World War II soldier, Desmond Doss, who ran into fields of mangled bodies and bloodied corpses to single-handedly save lives. While sitting in the theater, feeling as if a window to hell had been opened before me, I realized this is more than a film. A war is waging. It is one that is infinitely more ruthless, vicious and disturbing than anything that could be depicted on earth. We are living amidst a spiritual war with infinitely higher stakes. This battle is happening right now, without rest, without pity and without compassion. It is the war for your soul.

Scripture tells us that this war is not one that we can see with our eyes because it is against a hidden darkness (Eph. 6:12). Many say that Satan desires for people to believe that he isn't real because an enemy that isn't detected can easily attack. The first principle of war is that we know our enemy and how he will invade. The devil is the sly prince of lies who is "prowling like a roaring lion looking for someone to devour" (1 Pet. 5:8). We must be aware of the attempts and successes he has made in our lives in the past and then be on the lookout for ways he is tempting the culture around us. We mustn't think that our enemy doesn't also know this first principle. He knows his victims well and will always attack what he finds to be our weakest point. In turn, we must know ourselves in order to strengthen those areas of our hearts, minds, and souls that will be assaulted. It is only in understanding the threat and the urgency of this mission that one can begin to formulate a secure war strategy and defense.

Therefore, we must arm ourselves in the perfect and unfailing armor of God against the "tactics of the devil" (Eph 6:11). We can find rest and utter confidence in the fact that we are fighting on the winning side. It is sometimes thought that the devil is the opposite of God, but this simply isn't so. God is so much greater. The Lord is the Creator of all of the angels, of which Satan chose to fall away from. In trusting the Lord, arming ourselves within the Sacraments, reading the Word, seeking God's will and building our relationship to him and his Blessed Mother, we will become mighty warriors fully equipped to ride confidently into battle.

"Remember that one does not win the battle without prayer. The choice is yours." – St. Padre Pio

---

Prayers for Days 10-17 located on page 68

Daily Prayers for Days 10-17

Our Father...
Hail Mary...
Glory Be...

Prayer of Saint Francis
Lord, make me an instrument of your peace:
where there is hatred, let me sow love;
where there is injury, pardon;
where there is doubt, faith;
where there is despair, hope;
where there is darkness, light;
where there is sadness, joy.

O divine Master, grant that I may not so much seek
to be consoled as to console,
to be understood as to understand,
to be loved as to love.
For it is in giving that we receive,
it is in pardoning that we are pardoned,
and it is in dying that we are born to eternal life.
Amen.

Memorare
Remember, O most gracious Virgin Mary,
that never was it known that anyone who fled
to thy protection, implored thy help, or
sought thine intercession was left unaided.
Inspired by this confidence, I fly unto thee, O
Virgin of virgins, my mother; to thee do I

come, before thee I stand, sinful and
sorrowful. O Mother of the Word Incarnate,
despise not my petitions, but in thy mercy
hear and answer me. Amen.

Litany of the Holy Spirit

Lord Have Mercy on Us
Christ have Mercy on Us
Lord *Have Mercy on Us*
Father all powerful, *have mercy on us.*
Jesus Eternal Son of the Father, Redeemer of the World, *save us*
Spirit of the Father and the Son, boundless life of
both, *sanctify us.* Holy Trinity, *hear us*
Holy Spirit, Who proceeds from the Father and the Son *enter our hearts.*
Holy Spirit, Who is equal to the Father and the Son, *enter our hearts.*
Promise of God the Father, *have mercy on us.* Consuming
fire, *have mercy on us.*
Author of all good, *have mercy on us*
Ardent charity, *have mercy on us*
Spirit of love and truth, *have mercy on us*
Spirit of Wisdom and Understanding, *have mercy on us*
Spirit of Counsel and Fortitude, *have mercy on us*
Spirit of knowledge and Piety, *have mercy on us*
Spirit of Fear of the Lord, *have mercy on us*
Spirit of grace and prayer, *have mercy on us*
Sprit of peace and meekness, *have mercy on us*
Spirit of modesty and innocence, *have mercy on us*
Holy Spirit the comforter, *have mercy on us*
Holy Spirit, Who governs the Church, *have mercy on us*
Gift of God, the Most High, *have mercy on us*

Spirit Who fills the universe, *have mercy on us*

Holy Spirit, *inspire us with the horror of sin,*
Holy Spirit, *come and renew the face of the earth,*
Holy Spirit, *shed your light in our souls*
Holy Spirit, *engrave Your law in our hearts,*
Holy Spirit *inflame us with the flame of Your love,*
Holy Spirit, *open to us the treasures of Your graces,*
Holy Spirit, *teach us to pray well*
Holy Spirit, *lead us in the way of salvation*
Holy Spirit, *make us persevere in justice*
Holy Spirit, *be our everlasting reward*
Lamb of God you take away the sins of the world, *Send us Your Holy Spirit*

Lamb of God who takes away the sins of the world, Pour down into our souls the gifts of the Holy Spirit Lamb of God who takes away the sins of the world, *Grant us the Spirit of Wisdom and Piety*
V. Come, Holy Spirit! Fill the hearts of Your faithful.
R. *and enkindle in them the fire of Your love.*

Let Us Pray: Grant, O Merciful Father, that Your Divine Spirit may enlighten, inflame and purify us, that He may penetrate us with His heavenly dew and make us fruitful in good works, through Our Lord Jesus Christ, Your Son, Who with You, in the unity of the same Spirit, lives and reigns forever and ever. Amen

---

"You must speak to Jesus also with the heart, besides with the lips; indeed, in certain cases you must speak to Him only with the heart." - St. Padre Pio

---

Introduction to
Days 18-28

Our Lady

True devotion to Our Lady comes first from our mind and heart. Mary desires for us to have the confidence in her that a child has for its loving mother. As children, we run to our mother with **every** need with complete trust and affection. Having this confidence in Mary will surely lead to an avoidance of sin and an imitation of her virtues. Mary's example and our love for her can give us the courage and strength to approach the world and to avoid the seduction of the devil.

Pray that you will be rid of the fears that are holding you back so that you can give yourself freely to love her as Jesus did. In consecration, all we do will be perfected through Mary, with Mary, in Mary and for Mary – all for the purpose of giving glory to God. Remember that Jesus' body was formed in her womb, and he entered the world through her. Jesus becomes vulnerable in the womb of his Blessed Mother, depending on her for everything. In the mystery of the Incarnation, we find Jesus enveloped in Mary. We, therefore, thank God for the grace he gave Mary and in turn ask for the grace to grow in dependence on her.

Day 18

The Fall

Daily Reading: Genesis 3:1-15

In this third chapter of Genesis, we have been given the first prophesy in the Bible, and this story has set the stage for what is to come. God assures us that this woman will have enmity, meaning total opposition, with the devil. Through her offspring, she will crush the head of the serpent and be victorious. Sound familiar? We will see this theme played out as we come to understand God's providential plan for Mary and for the salvation of the world.

Our Mother is in complete opposition with Satan because she is full of humility. Satan, on the other hand, is full of pride. In fact, Mary is the most humble of all creatures, and we know from the Scriptures that it's the humble who will be exalted (Mt. 23:12). Satan is the most prideful of all creatures, so much so that it led to his rebellion. He despises that mere humans, who are far less intellectually capable than he, could be made in the image and likeness of God and share in the divinity of Christ. He cannot understand why an angel would be called upon to minister to lowly humans. He refuses. Simply put, Satan does not comprehend love and mercy. He is intellectually superior to us, but he has no wisdom.

Drawing near to Our Lady is our sure protection from the snares of the devil. St. Louis De Montfort teaches that Satan's pride causes him to flee at her presence. He knows she is triumphant over him, and therefore, he is unwilling to even put up a fight against her because she crushes his very head with her heel. Through the silence and the secret of her humility, Christ is always triumphant!

We should all take the example of Mary's humility as the virtue that we **must** possess before we can obtain any other. It is the virtue from which all others flow. When we seek to grow in humility, we come to a deeper understanding of who we are in respect to who God is.

"Humility is the highest of all human virtues."
- St. Francis de Sales

Prayers for Days 18-28 located on page 94

Day 19

The Virgin Prophesy

Daily Reading: Isaiah 7:14

Our God keeps his promises, and his will always prevails in the end. He guaranteed a deliverance from the sin of Adam and Eve (Gen. 3:14-15). The Lord promised that this anointed one, the Messiah, would come from the line of David (2 Sam. 7:12-16) and be born of a virgin (Is. 7:14). Of course, we know a virgin birth is impossible- it would take a miracle! The Gospel of Luke opens with the proclamation that this miracle has indeed taken place (Lk 1:26). Mary explains it herself! Clearly, the promise we hear in today's reading has been fulfilled in Mary.

What does Mary's virginity have to do with us? We learn from the Blessed Virgin Mother that perfect discipleship means giving the Lord *everything*. We all have a specific calling in our lives. Vocation means "total gift of self," which for some will be carried out in married or single life and for others in consecrated or religious life. In the vocation of marriage, the gift of the body is given exclusively to another. In religious vocations, men and women imitate Christ and his mother by offering their sexuality as a gift to God.

The important thing to remember is that regardless of our vocational call, our lives are always meant to be given to the Lord first. Our primary call is holiness, and our vocations serve this call as they carry us to Heaven. We look to Mary as our perfect example of complete self-gift. Through Marian Consecration, we will strive to give everything to Mary, so she can refine us and offer us to the Lord. Regardless of where God is calling you, let her example mold your inner purity in all areas of your life!

"All my own perception of beauty both in majesty and simplicity is founded upon Our Lady."
-J.R.R. Tolkien

Prayers for Days 18-28 located on page 94

Day 20

The Annunciation

Daily Reading: Luke 1:26-38

When you think of God's unrevealed plans for your life – what is your reaction? Fear? Anxiety? Apprehension? What if God asks you to do something you don't really want to do? What if God asks you to do something that doesn't even seem to make sense? Sometimes it is hard for us to *always want* to say yes to God.

The Annunciation is one of the most earth-shattering events in all of salvation history. The angel Gabriel appeared to Mary with the biggest question ever asked! Think about the significance of this event. What if she would have said no? All of creation, past, present and future, depended on her answer.

"Let it be done unto me accord to your will." That was the simple, humble and beautiful answer of Mary. Not only was this her answer to this particular question, but this is Mary's perpetual disposition. Her answer to God is always "Yes". Any time we see Mary move, she is only moving in submission to the will of God through the overshadowing of the Holy Spirit. Truly, when we see Mary, we see God's will in action.

We, too, must learn to hand ourselves over to the will of God. The simple and practical way of doing this is to pray the "Yes Prayer". Every morning before your feet hit the floor, tell God, "whatever you have for me today, the answer is *yes*." We simply tell God yes, all day, every day. We tell him yes to *anything* that he may will in our lives. When you say yes to the Lord in daily decisions, relationships, temptations, actions and words, it will slowly become the fabric of your very being. When we grow accustomed to saying yes to God in the small things, the big yeses will also come more naturally. Our Lord respects our free will to such a degree that he will never force anything upon us. Therefore, for him to freely accomplish all he wants from us, we must surrender ourselves over to his divine providence. Lord, let our wills become one with yours!

"Mary is the sanctuary and the repose of the Holy Trinity, where God dwells more magnificently and more divinely than in any other place in the universe." -St. Louis de Montfort

Prayers for Days 18-28 located on page 94

Day 21

The Visitation

Daily Reading: Luke 1:39-45

"How does this happen to me, that the mother of my Lord should come to me?" Imagine the joy that Elizabeth must have experienced as Mary came into her home. They had both recently conceived sons through miracles. Imagine the utter wonder, anticipation and contemplation of these two women preparing to give birth to the Savior and the one who would prepare his way.

When she heard Mary's voice, Elizabeth was filled with the Holy Spirit. The Holy Spirit entered into the depths of her so profoundly that the baby she carried in her womb leapt for joy. Of course, this baby was John the Baptist. Through the presence of Mary, the Holy Spirit filled the home and blessed the infant, John. Before he was even born, John was sanctified by Jesus through Mary. This is and always will be the only desire of Our Lady – to bring us to an encounter with her Son. This is the safest, easiest, shortest and most perfect pathway to sanctification – to Jesus through Mary. Mary brought Jesus to the world! Mary brought Jesus to Elizabeth and John. Mary will bring Jesus to us! Wherever we find her, we find Jesus working through the Holy Spirit. The Spirit never ceases to overshadow her. God didn't have to approach his people in this way- it wasn't a necessity. However, in his Divine wisdom and providence, he chose to give us this unique channel of holiness!

As we prepare to make our consecration, we also prepare to bring Our Lady into our homes and into our hearts. She will fill us with joy, fill us with the Holy Spirit and fill us with amazement just as she did for Elizabeth. We will feel the effects of her presence as John the Baptist did. In the home where Mary is welcomed, Jesus is always present!

"The Immaculata (Mary) is united to the Holy Spirit so closely that we really cannot grasp this union."
– St. Maximilian Kolbe

Prayers for Days 18-28 located on page 94

Day 22

The Magnificat

Daily Reading: Luke 1:46-56

This song of Mary in Scripture is called the Magnificat. It is her longest quoted statement in the entire Bible. Mary sings the praises of her Lord, God and Savior. She recognizes her own lowliness and humility. Mary recognizes the fact that God has indeed blessed her and done great things for her. She sings of his holiness and his mercy!

In all of her humility, Mary proclaims that all generations will call her blessed! This is an amazing proposition to say the least. Think about it: is there anyone you know who would say such a thing? What would we think of a person who made a claim like this one? The last thing on our mind would be the humility of this person. Nonetheless, Mary was perfectly humble as she uttered these bold words. She recognized that it was precisely her lowliness that would allow the Lord to work miraculous things in her.

Mary also reveals herself to be the handmaid of the Lord. This is a great insight indeed! Mary's life was spent in humble service of God. She served him in any way that he willed- both in his physical needs and his spiritual desires. Our Lady teaches us the secrets of the Father's heart. She illustrates that God looks upon and blesses those who live their lives as humble servants of their Savior. Let us live for this blessing that Mary reveals!

"Obedience unites us so closely to God that it in a way transforms us into him, so that we have no other will but his." - St. Thomas Aquinas

Prayers for Days 18-28 located on page 94

Day 23

The Nativity

Daily Reading: Luke 2:1-20

The scandal of the Incarnation should knock us to our knees. The reality that our God would become man and relate to our every need, struggle, temptation, suffering and even death is hard to fathom. God became man. The one who would redeem the whole world by his death and resurrection was "wrapped in swaddling clothes and lying in a manger" (Lk. 2:12).

Because Jesus was fully God and fully man, he was the only one who could restore the original harmony of creation. In Christ, spirit and matter are brought into perfect harmony. The divine and the human have come to reconciliation. We see this from the very moment of his birth, as all of creation rejoiced and praised this infant. Mary and Joseph, the Magi, the shepherds, the donkeys and oxen, the stars and the angels all gathered around the baby, Jesus. It was a glorious, silent night indeed! A night that changed the history of the world!

By Christ assuming human flesh, human nature was elevated even above the angels. What was once bound by time has now entered the timeless. Human nature is elevated into the heights of Divinity!

What must Mary have felt through all of this? In Scripture, she remains silent and speaks not a word. In our times, when a woman is pregnant, all of the attention is fixed on her. Yet, when she gives birth, the attention shifts and all gaze at the newborn life. The mother becomes secondary as everyone adores the baby – even the mother herself is captivated by the child. Mary surely was in adoration and contemplation from the moment of Jesus' birth, for she "kept all these things, reflecting on them in her heart" (Lk. 2:19). She brought Jesus to the world that day; she can bring Jesus into your world, today!

"The Mother of God cannot lead us anywhere except to the Lord Jesus." - St. Maximilian Kolbe

---

Prayers for Days 18-28 located on page 94

Day 24

The Prophesy of the Pierced Heart

Daily Reading: Luke 2:25-35

In today's reading, we see a great foreshadowing of what is to come. Imagine what Mary must have felt as Simeon spoke these words when he saw the infant Jesus, "My eyes have seen your salvation... This child is destined to cause the falling and rising of many in Israel... so that the thoughts of many hearts will be revealed." Mary and Joseph marveled as Simeon spoke these words. They were given the amazing opportunity to raise and to know the Salvation of the world, their very son, Jesus. Their hearts must have been overwhelmed with supernatural joy and wonder.

While this was the case, Simeon went on further to tell Mary that her heart would be pierced by a sword. When we read this, it seems strange. When we look through Scripture, we see that Mary's heart was never struck with a physical sword, but Jesus' was. After Jesus was already dead on the Cross, one of the soldiers pierced his heart with a sword and blood and water flowed out. The spiritual reality is that the Immaculate Heart of Mary and the Sacred Heart of Jesus are so closely united that one sword pierced both hearts. Mary experienced spiritually what Jesus experienced physically. The heart of Mary beats together with the heart of Jesus.

"This mother's heart is pierced to its very depths as she spiritually shares in the brutal immolation of her innocent son." - Dr. Mark Miravalle

Prayers for Days 18-28 located on page 94

Day 25

The Hidden Years

Daily Reading: Luke 2:51-52

From the ages of 12 to 30, we do not have an account of what took place in the lives of Jesus and Mary. What could have happened in these eighteen years of silence? How did they spend their days? Did Jesus perform miracles? Why the silence? Was there a secret?

The answer is yes! The secret of Nazareth is the secret of silence! There is power in silence. Silence and contemplation should always proceed work and action. Because God willed it, Jesus submitted himself to his mother. Not just until he was a teenager and not just until he turned eighteen or twenty-one, but for thirty years! We will see a clear example of this tomorrow.

We live in an action-packed world where our lives are filled with noise and busyness. Our world seeks productivity, efficiency and practicality. Often times, efficiency can be the enemy of charity. Even in our spiritual lives, we always feel the need to *do* and never a need to just *be*. While we *are* often called to action, we must understand and contemplate the importance of silence in our lives. The Christian life is more than outward actions. The origin of our Christian lives must be interior. While nothing extraordinary may have happened on the outside during the Holy Family's hidden years, everything was extraordinary on the inside! This always remains true of Mary, for all her glory is within.

In this Consecration, we must seek an interior silence and to set some time aside for prayer. If we are to grow in our relationship with

Christ and be fruitful in our actions, we must turn off some of the distractions in our lives and spend more silent time with God.

"In our time, Jesus also wants hidden saints...who distinguish themselves in nothing exteriorly, but who burn interiorly." – Father Jean C.J. d'Elbee

Prayers for Days 18-28 located on page 94

Day 26

The Feast of Cana

Daily Reading: John 2:1-11

Six ordinary stone jars, each holding twenty to thirty gallons, become extraordinary in today's story of the Wedding at Cana. Each of these jars were filled to the brim – truly a superabundance of wine! It's not just any wine, but Jesus gave them the good wine, the choice wine. The wedding of Cana was definitely a festive and joyful celebration... initiated at the request of Mary! Once again we see this pathway of *Jesus through Mary*.

This was the first public miracle of Jesus and thus began his public ministry. Through this miracle, he "revealed his glory and his disciples began to believe in him" (Jn 2:11). This was the beginning of #Jesusgoesviral in the Middle East. In this moment, he was well aware that his public ministry would lead to his death. The feast of the wedding of Cana would inevitably lead to the Cross, yet Mary and Jesus both knew it must take place. They understood that Christ must fulfill all things in himself and ultimately become the bread and wine of our salvation.

It is Mary who prepares us for this Eucharist as she recognizes that they have no wine. In this moment, she intercedes on behalf of humanity. The superabundance of wine that Jesus provides is a foreshadowing of what is to come – the Body and Blood of the new covenant. The water transformed into wine at the feast of Cana points us directly to the bread and wine transformed into the Body and Blood in the Eucharist. Christ once again provides us with a superabundance of the choice wine – a superabundance of himself. Christ is the choice wine, and Mary leads us to him once again with her last spoken words in Scripture, "Do whatever he tells you."

"To desire grace without recourse to the Virgin Mother is to desire to fly without wings." -Pope Pius XI

Prayers for Days 18-28 located on page 94

Day 27

The Cross

Daily Reading: John 19:25-27

It is hard to imagine the excruciating pain of Mary's heart as she witnessed her Son in his passion and death. Although, it was Jesus who was brutally crucified, she truly experienced a kind of death that day. We can only imagine what went through her mind as she looked at his crushed body and gazed into his eyes.

It was Mary who bore him in her womb for nine months and then brought him into the world. It was Mary who nursed him, taught him and raised him. It was Mary who lived with him for thirty years. It was Mary who initiated his public ministry. It was Mary who followed him all the way to the foot of the Cross and witnessed his death. It was her heart that was pierced by a sword. She contemplated the mystery of Christ more deeply than any other person in the history of Christianity. She understood the meaning of his life and death. She *really* knew him. As she gazed at him, all of this was in her mind and her heart. No person in the history of the world has ever gazed upon the face of Jesus Christ in the way that Mary has. No one has loved him with the intensity of his own mother.

"To contemplate the face of Christ, and to contemplate it with Mary is the program which I have set before the Church at the dawn of the third millennium." This is the pathway we have been given by Saint Pope John Paul II. To really know Christ and to experience him in the deepest and most profoundly real way, we are to gaze upon his face as Mary did. We are called to contemplate the face of Christ *with* Mary. This is the essence of all Marian devotion- to consecrate ourselves to this love of Jesus through the heart and eyes of his mother.

"God had one son on earth without sin, but never one without suffering." – St. Augustine

---

Prayers for Days 18-28 located on page 94

Day 28

The Battle

Daily Reading: Revelation 11:19, 12:17

Let us remember the reading from Day 18, when the serpent tricked Eve into eating the fruit. In today's reading, we see that the battle continues. In the first prophesy, God told the serpent, "I will put enmity between you and the woman, and between your offspring and hers" (Gen 3:15). The battle between the woman and the serpent begins from the onset of Scripture in Genesis and continues all the way to Revelation. The bookends of the Bible tell of this epic battle in Scripture, and it concludes as we see the woman crowned as Queen of Heaven and Earth.

"The woman" of Scripture is fulfilled in Mary. Mary is the new Eve because she is the new "mother of all the living" (Gen. 3:20). What Eve is in the order of nature, Mary is in the order of grace. Mary gave birth to the Savior of the world – the one who would triumph over the Devil once and for all. The Son, accompanied by his mother, restores all that was lost by the first man and woman. What Adam and Eve lost through disobedience, Jesus and Mary restored. They are the new Adam and the new Eve of the new creation.

Let's be clear, Jesus is Divine. Mary is not. Jesus was and is the one and only Redeemer of the world. Nonetheless, aren't we all called to participate in God's saving work? Eve was given the title of "helpmate," but fell short of fulfilling her role (Gen 2:18). Where

Eve failed, Mary succeeded. The Blessed Mother's continual goal was to submit to God in every moment. Her only desire was to be his helpmate – even unto the Cross. The new Eve isn't a bystander, but rather a cooperator in God's work of redemption.

In times of spiritual warfare, let us run to Our Lord and Our Lady. There is no reason to fear the evil one when they are at our side! Surely the head of the serpent will be crushed by them. The victory is already won for us- all we have to do is claim it!

"People ask me: 'What will convert America and save the world?' My answer is prayer. What we need is for every parish to come before Jesus in the Blessed Sacrament in Holy Hours of prayer."- Mother Teresa

---

Prayers for Days 18-28 located on page 95

Daily Prayers for Days 18-28

Pray one decade of the Rosary

Begin with one Our Father, followed by ten Hail Mary's and a Glory Be.

Note: If you're extra awesome and want to see multiple graces in your life, you could choose to pray a daily rosary during this section. For a step-by-step tutorial visit page 116. If you have fifteen minutes to bask in God's glory with Mary, then visit page 119 in the Appendix for our rosary reflections with the daily mysteries. As another alternative, you might be able to spare three minutes five times per day and split your rosary up over the course of your daily schedule. Perhaps you could pray one decade when you wake up, another on your way to school, one at lunch, one while walking to class and another before bed – suddenly you're meditating on Christ's life throughout the fabric of your entire day!

Litany of the Blessed Virgin Mary

Lord Have Mercy on Us *Christ have Mercy on Us*
Lord *Have Mercy on Us*
Christ Hear Us *Christ graciously hear us*
God the Father of Heaven, *Have Mercy on Us*
God the Son, Redeemer of the world, *Have Mercy on Us*
God the Holy Spirit, *Have Mercy on Us*
Holy Trinity, One God, *Have Mercy on Us*

Holy Mary, *pray for us*
Holy Mother of God, *pray for us*
Holy Virgin of virgins, *pray for us*
Mother of Christ, *pray for us* Mother most
pure, *pray for us* Mother most chaste, *pray
for us*
Mother most admirable. *pray for us*
Mother of good counsel. *pray for us*
Mother of our Creator, *pray for us*
Mother of our Savior, *pray for us*
Mother of the Church, *pray for us* Virgin most
prudent, *pray for us*
Virgin most powerful, *pray for us*
Virgin most merciful, *pray for us*
Virgin most faithful, *pray for us*
Cause of our joy, *pray for us*
Mystical rose, *pray for us*
Tower of David, *pray for us*
House of Gold, *pray for us*
Ark of the Covenant, *pray for us*
Gate of Heaven, *pray for us*
Morning Star, *pray for us*
Health of the sick, *pray for us*
Refuge of sinners, *pray for us*
Comforter of the afflicted, *pray for us*
Help of all Christians, *pray for us*
Queen of angels, *pray for us*
Queen of prophets, *pray for us*
Queen of Apostles, *pray for us*
Queen of martyrs, *pray for us*
Queen of virgins, *pray for us*

Queen of all saints, *pray for us*
Queen conceived without Original sin, *pray for us*
Queen assumed into Heaven, *pray for us*
Queen of the most holy rosary, *pray for us*
Queen of peace, *pray for us*

Lamb of God who takes away the sins of the world, *Spare us,
O Lord,*
Lamb of God, who takes away the sins of the world
Graciously hear, us O Lord
Lamb of God who Takes away the sins of the world, *have mercy on*
us
Pray for us O Holy Mother of God,
That we may be made worthy of the promises of Christ.

Let Us Pray
Grant we beseech Thee, O Lord God, unto us Your servants that
we may rejoice in continual health of mind and body, and by
glorious intercession of Blessed Mary, ever virgin, may be delivered
from present sadness, and enter into the joy of Your eternal
gladness. Through Christ Our Lord. *Amen*

Magnificat
My Soul does magnify the Lord.
And my spirit rejoices in God my Savior.
Because He has regarded the humility of His handmaid; for behold,
from henceforth all generation shall call me blessed.
Because He that is mighty has done great things to me, and holy is
His name.
And His Mercy is from generation to generation, to those that fear
Him.

He has shown might in His arm, He has scattered the proud in the conceit of their heart.

He has put down the might from their seat; and has exalted the humble.

He has filled the hungry with good things; and the rich he has sent empty away.

He has received Israel His servant, being mindful of His mercy.

As He spoke to our fathers, to Abraham and to his seed forever.

Amen

"Without contemplation, the Rosary is a body without a soul." - Pope Paul VI

Introduction to

Days 29-33

Our Lord

In these last days of preparation for Marian Consecration, our vision focuses on contemplating the face of Christ with Mary. Through this devotion, we will honor the dependence that Jesus chose to have on Mary. She is our ultimate example because she recognizes that she is who she is only by the grace and mercy of God. This is true humility. Mary cries out "My soul proclaims the greatness of the Lord" because she knew that her goodness came from him. And even more, she recognized that life is not about her at all but rather personally knowing Jesus Christ. It's about a relationship with him. It's about falling in love with him. It's about giving our lives to him. She knows her role. Mary simply brings souls to Christ and Christ to souls. He is the reason for this journey. He is what we have set out for. Jesus is everything!

Only in Jesus can we find the divinity and the fullness of grace, virtue and perfection. As St. Louis De Montefort says, "He is the teacher from whom we must learn; the only Lord on whom we should depend; the only one for us to imitate. He is the Physician that can heal us, the only Shepherd that can feed us, the only Way that can lead us, the only Truth that we can believe; the only Life that can animate us. He alone is everything to us and He alone can satisfy our desires."[4]

In these last few days, we will pray for the mercy of God to

---

[4] True Devotion to Mary Paragraph 61

guide us and shower upon us. We entrust ourselves to the Cross of Christ, knowing that his death has freed us and forgave us for our sins. In this time, we will pray not only for mercy on ourselves but for the whole world. Our culture is desperately in need of the mercy of God through Jesus Christ.

Day 29

The Word of God

Daily Reading: Deuteronomy 8:3 and Luke 4:1-4

Every human being is body and spirit composite. We *are* our bodies and we *are* our souls. This is what makes up our personhood and our entire self. To be fully alive and well, we must nourish both our body and our spirit. Therefore, it is good to eat nutritious foods, work out and even get the proper amount of sleep each night. These are all basic things that we should all do to take care of our bodies. What about our souls? What do you do daily to ensure that your soul thrives?

In the next three days, we will learn about the three foods that Christ provides us for our spiritual journey home to him. We will seek to live our lives by feeding on these foods and they will provide our souls with nourishment.

The first of these is the Word of God. When Satan tempted Jesus, Christ revealed Scripture to be spiritual food. The Scriptures are the very words that come from the mouth of God. Each time you read the Bible, Christ is *present* in your midst and he will surely speak to you. The Word of God penetrates the depths of who we are and stirs our hearts.

You have been feeding on the Word of God for twenty-nine days now and there is no question that God has spoken to your heart. Make a resolution to continue feeding your soul through this gift that God has given us. The hope is that this book with be a beginning of a life-long devotion and practice of prayer. Should we ever starve our bodies of nutrition we would die. How much more then should we feed our souls?

"The mind of the Scriptures can never be exhausted. It is a well without a bottom." - St. John Chrysostom

Prayers for Days 29-33 located on page 112

Day 30

The Will of God

Daily Reading: John 4:27-34

Christ reveals the second spiritual food to his Apostles as they try to offer him physical food to eat. Jesus says, "I have food to eat of which you do not know...my food is to do the will of him who sent me, and to accomplish his work" (Jn. 4:34). Jesus had no question about what his mission was. He also understood that it was this mission itself that would feed him.

Our souls are given real strength and are renewed when we seek to do the will of God. To the extent that we live our lives in the will of God is the extent that we will experience abundant life. The old fashion saying is true: the more we give the more we receive. The more we submit our will to his will, the more we will be fed. The hunger and thirst in our souls will be quenched.

We still may wonder, what is the will of God in my life? What does God desire of me? How does God desire for me to live? The answer is simple! "This is the will of God, your sanctification" (1 Thes. 4:3). The will of God is for us to be holy! Therefore, the will of God is to engage ourselves in things that are holy and thereby form us into the holy men and women he desires us to be!

Of course, this also means that the will of God is for us to avoid all things that lead us *away* from holiness. If you have hunger and thirst in your life, bravely and boldly ask the Lord to reveal the things that are dehydrating and malnourishing your soul. In turn, trust that he has the answers to satisfy you. The Author of all Creation wants to write a specific, beautiful story for your life. Jesus, we trust in you!

"Thoughtfulness is the beginning of great sanctity. If you learn this art of being thoughtful, you will become more and more Christlike, for His heart was meek and always thought of others." - St Teresa of Calcutta

Prayers for Days 29-33 located on page 112

Day 31

The Eucharist

Daily Reading: John 6:22-71

This reading speaks for itself. Jesus tells the crowd over and over and over again that his Body and Blood are truly food and drink. In John 6:66 (the only 6:66 passage in the Bible), it says that people began to leave because of this outrageous teaching. If Jesus was speaking symbolically, then of course he would have explained the analogy to keep his followers and friends. Instead, he insists even further that he literally is the Bread of Life and that we must eat his flesh. When we read this passage from John, we should greatly appreciate the Catholic faith. Jesus wants to be so close to us that his blood mingles with ours.

Our ultimate spiritual food and drink is the Eucharist: The Body, Blood, Soul, and Divinity of Christ. The Eucharist is 100% Jesus Christ himself. He is as real to us as he was to the Apostles who spoke to him face to face. In the Eucharist, we feed on Jesus himself. This is certainly the climactic spiritual experience we get to experience on earth!

St. Leo the Great says, "The partaking of the Body and Blood of Christ does nothing other than to cause us to be transformed into that which we consume." This food is meant not only to nourish us but to *transform* us into him. Jesus Christ comes into the depths of who we are and transforms us from the inside out.

When we receive the Eucharist, we become walking tabernacles as we hold the body of Christ within us. Let's ask Mary to help us receive the Lord's body as perfectly as she did in order to bring him to the world.

"If the Angels could envy, they would envy us for Holy Communion." – Pope Pius X

Prayers for Days 29-33 located on page 112

Day 32

Adoration

Daily Reading: Revelation 7: 9-17

Adoration is the elementary point of our spiritual lives. In other words, it is the most fundamental and foundational point. The act of adoration is simply to place ourselves within God's presence, accept his great love for us and surrender ourselves to his providence. In adoration, we contemplate Jesus' desire to be intimate with us to the depths of our being. He possesses us more than we possess ourselves.

Jesus speaks to us, educates us and reveals spiritual matters to us through adoration. Jesus always speaks to us with a still, small voice. Only when we enter the desert of adoration, only when we simplify and quiet down our busy lives will we begin to effectively hear the voice of God. The silence of adoration quiets the constant chatter we fill ourselves with. We sometimes fear the silence because we are accustomed to the noise but the distractions block the voice of God. We need this deep and interior silence. Jesus is always patiently waiting for this encounter and is *longing* to speak to us.

When we adore the Lord, we receive "the peace of Christ, that surpasses all understanding" (Phil. 4:7). We are no longer anxious with the bombardment of drama and stress of daily life. When we live in adoration, we no longer have one eye fixed on Christ and the other on the world. Therefore, we are liberated and experience profound freedom! When we adore, we fix our eyes completely on Jesus— just as our Mother always had her eyes on her son— and all else fades away. It's not that the problems of the world no longer exist or that the to-do-list is any shorter, but our disposition completely changes when we learn to give thanks and praise in all circumstances. We begin to embody an attitude of trust and thus walk in the freedom he desires for us. In adoration, we stare at him, and he stares at us. His gaze penetrates the depths of us and purifies those areas that we don't want anyone else to see. It makes sense that in this adoration of Christ we discover what we are created for!

"Man should tremble, the world should vibrate, all Heaven should be deeply moved when the Son of God appears on the altar in the hands of the priest."
- St. Francis of Assisi

Prayers for Days 29-33 located on page 112

Day 33

Behold Thy Mother

Daily Reading: John 19:25-27

Use today's reflection as a meditation and really place yourself in this scripture passage as the beloved disciple. It was intended to be so because *you are his beloved disciple*. Yes, this story is about you.

There you are, at the foot of the Cross with Mary, witnessing the final moments in the life of Jesus. There is chaos all around but your gaze is fixed solely on him and you are so consumed that you don't even realize the noise all around you It is the most intense moment of your entire life. Jesus is staring back at you. Despite all his pain, his face is still full of love, mercy and compassion. Take a break and close your eyes. Breathe in the gravity of this moment.

When a person is crucified, they die from something called asphyxiation. Jesus' lungs slowly filled with fluid and he eventually suffocated. It was a slow and excruciating process. Jesus would have had to press down on his pierced feet to raise his chest enough to gasp for ample oxygen to speak. His words at the Cross are so few, and each one would cost a great deal of pain as it left his lips.

As you kneel at the foot of the cross, Jesus slowly appears as if he is going to speak to you. What will he say? You wonder, "Jesus is dying on the Cross and he wants to speak to me? He is in all this pain, yet he wishes to tell me something? This must be very important, maybe the most important secret that he has waited to tell me until now." His mother, Mary, is right beside you, anticipating his words as well.

Jesus gazes into your eyes, his disciple, and he slowly opens his mouth and says, **"Behold, thy mother."**

As Jesus gives his everything, he holds onto his precious mother until the very end. As his final gift before his death, Jesus gives you the Queen of his heart and trusts you to make her the Queen of yours.

"From that hour the disciple took her into his home."

-John 19:27

Final Consecration Prayer

Sweet and Holy Jesus, I come before you now in humility. You are the Lord, the maker of all things and the true King of the Universe and my heart. You chose a humble handmaid as your pathway into this world. Thank you for making yourself vulnerable to Mary through the Incarnation. I am grateful for your gift of Mary to the world.

Jesus, I confess that I have not kept my baptismal vows. Often times I have said yes to sin and no to you. Like the prodigal son, I feel that I do not deserve to approach you. Because I find myself unworthy and ashamed, I do not wish to walk to you alone. I have chosen to surrender myself to the Blessed Mother and walk with her to the Heavenly Banquet that you have offered to this poor soul. I desire to take Mary into my heart and my home just as St. Joseph did in Nazareth and St. John did at the foot of the cross.

I turn to you Mary, you who were a physical tabernacle for nine months, and I ask that I may better understand the presence of Christ in me. You who are virtuous, beautiful, humble, sinless and Immaculate, be my mother and my example. I am humbly confident in you, Virgin of Virgins, my Mother.

I, (insert name), am a reckless sinner who wishes to renew and confirm the promises I have made in my baptism. I will reject Satan and his empty promises. I will turn my eyes always to the crucified Christ and will follow his footsteps to Calvary. I will earnestly try to sin no more and be faithful in all I do.

I choose you, Mary, as my mother, and I give myself to you with the aspiration of arriving at Christ. I consecrate all of myself to you. I will hold nothing back in regards to possessions, both spiritual and material, and merits, past, present and future. I trust that all of this will be done for the greater glory of God and my own sanctification.

Mary, I find myself eternally grateful for all that the Lord has given to you, and I will try to honor and obey you in all things. We have received Christ through you and it is my desire that he will receive me in the same way. Take me as your child and make me overflow with the fullness of what God has desired and designed for me.

Totus Tuus! I am totally yours. Oh Mary, give me your heart to love Jesus more!

Amen.

Signature:
_____

Date
_____

Daily Prayers for Days 29-33

Divine Mercy Chaplet

Using Rosary beads, follow the same format as the rosary with the modifications below:

1. Begin with the Sign of the Cross, one Our Father, one Hail Mary and The Apostles Creed.

2. On Our Father Beads say: Eternal Father, I offer You the Body and Blood, Soul and Divinity of Your dearly beloved Son, Our Lord Jesus Christ, in atonement for our sins and those of the whole world.

3. On the ten Hail Mary Beads say: For the sake of His sorrowful Passion, have mercy on us and on the whole world.

4. Conclude with *(three times)*:
Holy God, Holy Mighty One, Holy Immortal One, have mercy on us and on the whole world.

Litany of the Holy Name of Jesus

Lord, have mercy on us.
Christ, have mercy on us.
Lord, have mercy on us. Jesus, hear us.
Jesus, graciously hear us.
God the Father of Heaven
Have mercy on us.
God the Son, Redeemer of the world,
Have mercy on us.

God the Holy Spirit,
Have mercy on us.
Holy Trinity, one God,
Jesus, Son of the living God, *have mercy on us*
Jesus, splendor of the Father, *have mercy on us*
Jesus, brightness of eternal light, *have mercy on us*
Jesus, King of glory, *have mercy on us*
Jesus, sun of justice, *have mercy on us*
Jesus, Son of the Virgin Mary, *have mercy on us*
Jesus, most amiable, *have mercy on us*
Jesus, most admirable, *have mercy on us*
Jesus, the mighty God, *have mercy on us*
Jesus, Father of the world to come, *have mercy on us*
Jesus, angel of great counsel, *have mercy on us*
Jesus, most powerful, *have mercy on us*
Jesus, most patient, *have mercy on us*
Jesus, most obedient, *have mercy on us*
Jesus, meek and humble of heart, *have mercy on us*
Jesus, lover of chastity, *have mercy on us*
Jesus, lover of us, *have mercy on us*
Jesus, God of peace, *have mercy on us*
Jesus, author of life, *have mercy on us*
Jesus, example of virtues, *have mercy on us*
Jesus, zealous lover of souls, *have mercy on us*
Jesus, our God, *have mercy on us*
Jesus, our refuge, *have mercy on us*
Jesus, father of the poor, *have mercy on us*
Jesus, treasure of the faithful, *have mercy on us*
Jesus, good Shepherd, *have mercy on us*
Jesus, true light, *have mercy on us*
Jesus, eternal wisdom, *have mercy on us*
Jesus, infinite goodness, *have mercy on us*
Jesus, our way and our life, *have mercy on us*

Jesus, joy of Angels, *have mercy on us*
Jesus, King of the Patriarchs, *have mercy on us*
Jesus, Master of the Apostles, *have mercy on us*
Jesus, teacher of the Evangelists, *have mercy on us*
Jesus, strength of Martyrs, *have mercy on us*
Jesus, light of Confessors, *have mercy on us*
Jesus, purity of Virgins, *have mercy on us*
Jesus, crown of Saints, *have mercy on us*

Be merciful, *spare us, O Jesus.*
Be merciful, *graciously hear us, O Jesus.*

From all evil, *deliver us, O Jesus*
From all sin, *deliver us, O Jesus*
From Your wrath, *deliver us, O Jesus*
From the snares of the devil, *deliver us, O Jesus*
From the spirit of fornication, *deliver us, O Jesus*
From everlasting death, *deliver us, O Jesus*
From the neglect of Your inspirations, *deliver us, O Jesus*
By the mystery of Your holy Incarnation, *deliver us, O Jesus*
By Your Nativity, *deliver us, O Jesus*
By Your Infancy, *deliver us, O Jesus*
By Your most divine Life, *deliver us, O Jesus*
By Your labors, *deliver us, O Jesus*
By Your agony and passion, *deliver us, O Jesus*
By Your cross and dereliction, *deliver us, O Jesus*
By Your sufferings, *deliver us, O Jesus*
By Your death and burial, *deliver us, O Jesus*
By Your Resurrection, *deliver us, O Jesus*
By Your Ascension, *deliver us, O Jesus*
By Your institution of the most Holy Eucharist, *deliver us, O Jesus*
By Your joys, *deliver us, O Jesus*
By Your glory, *deliver us, O Jesus*

Lamb of God, who takes away the sins of the world, *spare us, O Jesus.*
Lamb of God, who takes away the sins of the world, *graciously hear us, O Jesus.*
Lamb of God, who takes away the sins of the world, *have mercy on us, O Jesus.*

Jesus, hear us.
Jesus, graciously hear us.

Let us pray.

O Lord Jesus Christ, You have said, "Ask and you shall receive, seek, and you shall find, knock, and it shall be opened to you." Grant, we beg of You, to us who ask it, the gift of Your most divine love, that we may ever love You with our whole heart, in word and deed, and never cease praising You.

Give us, O Lord, as much a lasting fear as a lasting love of Your Holy Name, for You, who live and are King for ever and ever, never fail to govern those whom You have solidly established in Your love. Amen.

"And even if the sins of soul are as dark as night, when the sinner turns to my mercy he gives me the greatest praise and is the glory of My Passion." -Jesus to St Faustina

---

Appendix

How to Pray the Rosary

1. Make the Sign of the Cross.
2. Holding the Crucifix, say the *Apostles' Creed*- I believe in God, the Father Almighty, Creator of Heaven and earth; and in Jesus Christ, His only Son Our Lord, who was conceived by the Holy Spirit, born of the Virgin Mary, suffered under Pontius Pilate, was crucified, died, and was buried. He descended into Hell; the third day he rose again from the dead; he ascended into Heaven, and sits at the right hand of God, the Father almighty; from thence he shall come to judge the living and the dead. I believe in the Holy Spirit, the holy Catholic Church, the communion of saints, the forgiveness of sins, the resurrection of the body and life everlasting. Amen.
3. On the first bead, say an *Our Father:* Our Father, who art in heaven, hallowed be thy name. Thy Kingdom come. Thy will be done, on earth as it is in Heaven. Give us this day our daily bread and forgive us our trespasses, as we forgive those who trespass against us. Lead us not into temptation, but deliver us from evil. Amen.
4. Say one *Hail Mary* on each of the next three beads: Hail Mary Full of grace the Lord is with you. Blessed are you among women and blessed is the fruit of your womb, Jesus. Holy Mary, Mother of God, pray for us sinners, now and at the hour of our death. Amen.
5. Say the *Glory Be:* Glory Be to the Father, the Son and the Holy Spirit. As it was in the beginning is now and ever shall be, world without end. Amen

6. For each of the five decades, announce the Mystery (listed below) then say the *Our Father*.
7. While fingering each of the ten beads of the decade, next say ten *Hail Marys* while meditating on the Mystery. (If desired, you can pray our bead-by-bead meditations beginning on page 119)
8. After completion of each set of ten Hail Mary's, say a *Glory Be*.
9. After finishing each decade, some say the following prayer requested by the Blessed Virgin Mary at Fatima: *O my Jesus, forgive us our sins, save us from the fires of hell; lead all souls to Heaven, especially those who have most need of your mercy.*
10. After saying the five decades, say the *Hail, Holy Queen*: Hail, holy Queen, Mother of mercy, hail, our life, our sweetness, and our hope. To thee do we cry, poor banished children of Eve: to thee do we send up our sighs, mourning and weeping in this vale of tears. Turn then, most gracious Advocate, thine eyes of mercy toward us, and after this our exile, show unto us the blessed fruit of thy womb, Jesus, O merciful, O loving, O sweet Virgin Mary! Amen.
11. Conclude with the following prayer: Pray for us, O holy Mother of God, that we may be made worthy of the promises of Christ. *Let us pray: O God, whose Only Begotten Son, by his life, Death, and Resurrection, has purchased for us the rewards of eternal life, grant, we beseech thee, that while meditating on these mysteries of the most holy Rosary of the Blessed Virgin Mary, we may imitate what they contain and obtain what they promise, through the same Christ our Lord. Amen.*

The Mysteries of the Rosary and Their Fruits

The rosary is meant to be a concrete way for us to meditate on Jesus' life with Mary. Rather than thinking about the words of the Hail Mary, we are encouraged to contemplate the Mysteries of the life of Christ and let them sink into our hearts! Also listed below are the fruits of the mysteries or affects we hope these meditations will have in our own lives.

Joyful Mysteries (Monday, Saturday)

1. The Annunciation (of the Birth of the Savior to Mary): Humility
2. The Visitation (of Mary to Elizabeth and John the Baptist): Charity, Love of neighbor
3. The Nativity of Our Lord: Poverty of spirit, Detachment from the things of the world, Contempt of riches, Love of the poor
4. The Presentation of Jesus at the Temple: Obedience, Purity of intention
5. The Finding of the Child Jesus in the Temple: Piety

Sorrowful Mysteries (Tuesday, Friday)

1. The Agony in the Garden: Contrition, Conformity to the will of God
2. The Scourging at the Pillar: Purity, Mortification
3. The Crowning with Thorns: Moral Courage, Contempt of the world
4. The Carrying of the Cross: Patience
5. The Crucifixion: Final perseverance, Salvation, Self-Denial

Glorious Mysteries (Sunday, Wednesday)

1. The Resurrection: Faith
2. The Ascension: Hope, Desire for Heaven
3. The Descent of the Holy Spirit (on Mary and the Apostles at Pentecost): Love of God, Wisdom, Knowing and sharing the truth

4. The Assumption of Mary: Devotion to Mary, Grace of a happy death
5. The Coronation of the Blessed Virgin Mary: Eternal Happiness

Luminous Mysteries (Thursday)

1. The Baptism of Jesus in the Jordan: Openness to the Holy Spirit, Living one's baptismal promises
2. The Miracle at Cana: To Jesus through Mary, Doing whatever Jesus says
3. The Proclamation of the Kingdom of God: Repentance, Trust in God
4. The Transfiguration: Becoming a new person in Christ, Desire for holiness
5. The Institution of the Eucharist: Eucharistic Adoration, Active participation at Mass

Bead-by-Bead Rosary Mediations

Sometimes it is easy for our minds to wander during prayer. These meditations will give you a snippet of the mystery to think about for each Hail Mary, making it easy for those of us with short attention spans to stay on track!

These snippets are adapted from St. Louis De Montfort's 'A Method of Saying the Most Holy Rosary.'

The Joyful Mysteries
1. The Annunciation

- To remember the condemnation of Adam's disobedience that fell on all his descendants. *Hail Mary...*
- To honor the desires of the Old Testament peoples waiting for the Messiah. *Hail Mary...*
- To honor Mary's desire and prayers for the coming of the Savior
- To honor Mary's marriage to St. Joseph. *Hail Mary...*
- In contemplation of the Eternal Father giving us His Son. *Hail Mary...*
- In contemplation of the love of the son who gave himself up for us. *Hail Mary...*
- In contemplation of the mission and greeting of the angel, Gabriel. *Hail Mary...*
- To honor the faith and "yes" of the Virgin Mary. *Hail Mary...*
- In contemplation of the creation of the soul and formation of the body of Jesus in the womb of Mary by the Holy Spirit. *Hail Mary...*
- In honor of the majesty of God. *Hail Mary...*

2. The Visitation
- To honor the heart of Mary during Christ's dwelling for nine months. *Hail Mary...*
- To honor the sacrifice of himself that Jesus offering in coming into the world. *Hail Mary...*
- To honor the contentment of Jesus within Mary. *Hail Mary...*
- In contemplation of Joseph on discovering Mary's pregnancy. *Hail Mary...*

- To honor St. Joseph's trust in God. *Hail Mary...*
- In contemplation of Mary's excitement in visiting her cousin. *Hail Mary...*
- In honor of the greeting of Mary and the sanctification of St. John the Baptist. *Hail Mary...*
- In honor of Mary's song of thanksgiving to God in her Magnificat. *Hail Mary...*
- In honor of the charity and humility as Mary served her cousin. *Hail Mary...*
- In honor of the dependence of Jesus on Mary and the dependence we should have on them both. *Hail Mary...*

3. The Nativity
    - To remember the trip of the pregnant Mary on a donkey to Bethlehem. *Hail Mary...*
    - To remember the unpleasant cave when there was no room for the Christ to be born. *Hail Mary...*
    - In recollection of the exceeding love of Mary as she was about to give birth to Jesus. *Hail Mary...*
    - In honor of St. Joseph's awe as he preparing to meet his son and Savior. *Hail Mary...*
    - In contemplation of the birth of Jesus. *Hail Mary...*
    - In contemplation of the first moment that Mary and Jesus saw one another. *Hail Mary...*
    - In honor of the adoration and singing of the angels when Jesus was born. *Hail Mary...*
    - In contemplation of the beauty of her divine child. *Hail Mary...*

- To remember the coming of the shepherds with their humble gifts. *Hail Mary…*
- In contemplation of the Wise Men seeking the Redeemer. *Hail Mary…*

4. The Presentation
- In honor of Mary and Joseph's obedience to the law. *Hail Mary…*
- In honor of the circumcision of Jesus and his suffering accepted in love. *Hail Mary…*
- In honor of the giving of the name, Jesus. *Hail Mary…*
- Joining in the joy and songs of Simeon and Anna. *Hail Mary…*
- To remember the massacre of the Holy Innocents by Herod. *Hail Mary…*
- In remembrance of the flight of Jesus to Egypt though St. Joseph's obedience to the angel. *Hail Mary…*
- In contemplation of the mystery of Jesus' time in Egypt. *Hail Mary…*
- In remembrance of the Holy Family's return to Nazareth. *Hail Mary…*
- To honor Christ's hidden, hardworking and obedient life at Nazareth. *Hail Mary…*
- In contemplation of Jesus' growth in age and wisdom. *Hail Mary…*

5. The Finding of Jesus in the Temple
- To remember the anxiety of Mary and Joseph when they took their eyes of Jesus. *Hail Mary…*
- To remember the search for Jesus. *Hail Mary…*

- In contemplation of the joy at finding the Lord. *Hail Mary…*
- In honor of the holy words of God. *Hail Mary…*
- To remember the teaching of Jesus. *Hail Mary…*
- To remember that Jesus will always be found in his Father's house. *Hail Mary…*
- In honor of the amazement at Jesus' wisdom. *Hail Mary…*
- In contemplation of the burning of the hearts of those who heard Jesus preach. *Hail Mary…*
- In honor of Jesus' youth at the time of this witness. *Hail Mary…*
- In contemplation of the hidden years of the Holy Family. *Hail Mary…*

The Sorrowful Mysteries
1. The Agony in the Garden
   - In contemplation of Jesus' patience with his apostles during his life and especially in the Garden. *Hail Mary…*
   - To remember Jesus' contemplation of your face as he gathered the strength to endure his passion. *Hail Mary…*
   - In honor of the sweating of blood in which his sorrows bathed him. *Hail Mary…*
   - In contemplation of the comfort he took from the angel that consoled him. *Hail Mary…*
   - In honor of his willingness to follow the will of God beyond what his human reluctance. *Hail Mary…*

- In contemplation of the courage with which he went to meet his executioners. *Hail Mary...*
- In contemplation of the betrayal of Judas and the arrest by the Jews. *Hail Mary...*
- In remembrance of his desertion by his apostles. *Hail Mary...*
- To honor the chains and ropes with which he was bound. *Hail Mary...*
- In contemplation of the loneliness of Jesus in his cell awaiting his trial. *Hail Mary...*

2. The Scourging at the Pillar
- In remembrance of the three denials of Peter. *Hail Mary...*
- In remembrance of his shameful treatment at the house of Herod, *Hail Mary...*
- In contemplation of his being stripped of his clothes. *Hail Mary...*
- In contemplation of the scorn and insults he received. *Hail Mary...*
- In memory of his beating with the cat of nine tails. *Hail Mary...*
- In honor of the pillar to which he was bound. *Hail Mary...*
- In honor of the blood he shed and the wounds he received, *Hail Mary...*
- In contemplation of his collapse into a pool of his own blood, *Hail Mary...*
- In contemplation of his mother watching his beating, *Hail Mary...*

- In contemplation of his beauty even in his brokenness, *Hail Mary...*

3. The Crowning of Thorns
   - In honor of the veil with which they blindfolded him, *Hail Mary...*
   - In contemplation of the blows and spittle that rained on his face, *Hail Mary...*
   - In honor of the robe they placed on his shoulders, *Hail Mary...*
   - In remembrance of the reed they put in his hand, *Hail Mary...*
   - In remembrance of the abuse and insults hurled at him, *Hail Mary...*
   - In contemplation of the thorns that thrust into his skin, *Hail Mary...*
   - In honor of the blood that poured from his head, *Hail Mary...*
   - To remember his hair and beard which they tore at, *Hail Mary...*
   - To remember his presentation to the people when Pilate said, "Behold the Man," *Hail Mary...*
   - In memory of the crowds yelling, "Crucify him," *Hail Mary...*

4. The Carrying of the Cross
   - In memory of the false testimonies given against him, *Hail Mary...*
   - To remember his being condemned to death, *Hail Mary...*
   - In honor of the love with which he embraced and kissed the Cross, *Hail Mary...*

- In honor of the suffering he endured while carrying it, *Hail Mary...*
- In contemplation of his falling through weakness under its weight, *Hail Mary...*
- In memory of the insults from the soldiers and crowds, *Hail Mary...*
- In honor of his sorrow when meeting his mother, *Hail Mary...*
- In honor of the veil of Veronica, *Hail Mary...*
- To memory of Simon carrying his cross alongside him, *Hail Mary...*
- In honor of the tears of his mother and the women who followed him to Calvary, *Hail Mary...*

5. The Crucifixion
- In honor of the nails and lance that pierced him, *Hail Mary...*
- To remember the shameful nature of execution by crucifixion, *Hail Mary...*
- To honor the compassion of the Blessed Mother, *Hail Mary...*
- In honor of his seven last words, *Hail Mary...*
- In honor of his silence, *Hail Mary...*
- In memory of the distress of the whole universe, *Hail Mary...*
- In contemplation of his painful and shameful death, *Hail Mary...*
- In honor of his final breath, *Hail Mary...*
- In contemplation of being taken down from the cross and his burial, *Hail Mary...*

- In contemplation of the decent of his soul into the dead, *Hail Mary…*

The Luminous Mysteries
1. The Baptism in the Jordan
   - In contemplation of John the Baptist's recognition of the Messiah, *Hail Mary…*
   - In honor of Jesus' desire for Baptism, *Hail Mary…*
   - In honor of Jesus' entry into the Jordan River, *Hail Mary…*
   - In contemplation of Jesus' descent into the depths of the waters of creation, *Hail Mary…*
   - To honor his saving power, *Hail Mary…*
   - In contemplation of his emergence from the Jordan, *Hail Mary…*
   - In honor of this descent and rising as it foreshadows his death and resurrection, *Hail Mary…*
   - To remember the voice of God saying, "This is my Beloved Son, with whom I am well pleased," *Hail Mary…*
   - In honor of the descent of the Holy Spirit upon Jesus, *Hail Mary…*
   - In thanksgiving for the moment of our own Baptism, *Hail Mary…*
2. The Wedding at Cana
   - To remember the couple who had the Messiah present at their wedding, *Hail Mary…*

- To remember of the areas of our life where we fall short and need Jesus' intercession, *Hail Mary...*
- In contemplation of Mary's knowledge that this would mark the end of their hidden life together, *Hail Mary...*
- In contemplation of the ordinary becoming extraordinary, *Hail Mary...*
- In honor of Mary's response to the prompting of the Holy Spirit, *Hail Mary...*
- In honor of Jesus' cooperation with Mary, *Hail Mary...*
- In honor of the servants doing whatever he told them, *Hail Mary...*
- To remember the joy of the guests in Cana, *Hail Mary...*
- In contemplation of the awe of the people who began to ask, "Who is this man?" *Hail Mary...*
- In thanksgiving for the superabundance of God, *Hail Mary...*

3. The Proclamation of the Kingdom
    - In thanksgiving for the Word of God that is fruitful and alive, *Hail Mary...*
    - To remember Jesus' call to deeper conversion and relationship with God, *Hail Mary...*
    - In contemplation of what it means to be poor in spirit, for theirs is the kingdom of Heaven, *Hail Mary...*
    - In contemplation of what it means to mourn, for they shall be comforted, *Hail Mary...*

- In contemplation of what it means to be meek, for they shall inherit the earth, *Hail Mary…*
- In contemplation of what it means to hunger and thirst for righteousness, for they shall be satisfied, *Hail Mary…*
- In contemplation of what it means to be merciful, for they shall obtain mercy, *Hail Mary…*
- In contemplation of what it means to be pure of heart, for they shall see God, *Hail Mary…*
- In contemplation of what it means to be a peacemaker, for they shall be called children of God, *Hail Mary…*
- In contemplation of what it means to be persecuted for the sake of righteousness, for theirs is the kingdom of heaven, *Hail Mary…*

4. The Transfiguration
   - In contemplation of Peter, James and John's intimate encounter with Christ, *Hail Mary…*
   - In honor of the light that shattered the ordinary appearance of daily life, *Hail Mary…*
   - In contemplation of the shining face of Jesus, *Hail Mary…*
   - In honor of the presence of Moses and Elijah, *Hail Mary…*
   - In honor of the voice of God proclaiming, "This is my Beloved Son. Listen to him," *Hail Mary…*
   - In contemplation of the Apostles' fear of the Lord, *Hail Mary…*

- In contemplation of the joy of the Apostles and the desire to remain in this moment of glory, *Hail Mary...*
- In thanksgiving that the Apostles weren't meant to dwell in the experience but the experience was meant to dwell in them, *Hail Mary...*
- To remember our own "mountain-top" experiences with the Lord, *Hail Mary...*
- In honor of God's glory, *Hail Mary...*

5. The Institution of the Eucharist
   - In honor of the gathering to celebrate the Passover, *Hail Mary...*
   - In contemplation of Jesus' desire to give of himself so deeply, *Hail Mary...*
   - In contemplation of the moment Jesus holds his heart in his hands and breaks it for our salvation, *Hail Mary...*
   - In honor of the chalice holding the blood of our salvation, *Hail Mary...*
   - In contemplation of the vulnerability of Jesus in his Eucharistic Presence on earth, *Hail Mary...*
   - To remember how the Apostles would recognize the Risen Christ later "in the breaking of the bread," *Hail Mary...*
   - In contemplation of Jesus' desire to dwell so intimately within us, *Hail Mary...*
   - To remember the time spent alone in the tabernacle, *Hail Mary...*
   - In thanksgiving for the Eucharist as the source and summit of our faith, *Hail Mary...*

- To ask Mary to help us hold Christ within us as gracefully as she did, *Hail Mary...*

The Glorious Mysteries

1. Resurrection

   - In contemplation of the cold, dark lifeless tomb, *Hail Mary...*
   - In contemplation of the reuniting of his body and soul, *Hail Mary...*
   - In contemplation of that first breath, *Hail Mary...*
   - In honor of his emergence from the tomb, *Hail Mary...*
   - In memory of his appearance to his mother, apostles and disciples, *Hail Mary...*
   - In honor of the power that he received from his Father, *Hail Mary...*
   - To remember the emotion of those who saw him risen, *Hail Mary...*
   - To remember the meal he shared with the disciples, *Hail Mary...*
   - In honor of the limitless power of God, *Hail Mary...*
   - In honor of the reality that Jesus shared our punishment, but also his reward, *Hail Mary...*

2. The Ascension

   - To remember the gathering of Christ with his Apostles as they prepare for his Ascension, *Hail Mary...*
   - In contemplation of the call of evangelization given to the Apostles, *Hail Mary...*

- To honor the dignity of the mission of the Apostles which is passed down to us, *Hail Mary...*
- In contemplation of the wonder and awe of the Apostles as they witnessed the Ascension, *Hail Mary...*
- In honor of the blessings he gave them as he rose to heaven, *Hail Mary...*
- To remember the rejoicing of the angels in this moment of glory, *Hail Mary...*
- In contemplation of the triumphant power with which he opened the gates of Heaven, *Hail Mary...*
- In honor of the justice he exercised at the judgment of the living and the dead, *Hail Mary...*
- In honor of Jesus' seat at the right hand of the Father, *Hail Mary...*
- To remember the emotion of the Apostles as they went forth from this moment, *Hail Mary...*

3. The Pentecost
- To remember the descent of the Holy Spirit, *Hail Mary...*
- To remember the rush of the great wind, *Hail Mary...*
- In contemplation of the tongues of fire, *Hail Mary...*
- In honor of the gift to the apostles giving them wisdom, understanding, counsel, fortitude, knowledge, piety, and fear of the Lord, *Hail Mary...*

- In honor of the fullness of grace received in the heart of Mary, *Hail Mary…*
- In honor of the guidance of the saints given by the Holy Spirit, *Hail Mary…*
- To ask for the coming of the Spirit into our heart's today, *Hail Mary…*
- To ask for victory of the Holy Spirit over the flesh, the world and the devil, *Hail Mary…*
- In thanksgiving for the gift of Confirmation, *Hail Mary…*
- In honor of the unspeakable generosity of God, *Hail Mary…*

4. The Assumption of Mary
   - In honor of Mary's birth that gladdened the whole world, *Hail Mary…*
   - In honor of her presentation in the temple, *Hail Mary…*
   - In contemplation of Mary's wonderful sinless life, *Hail Mary…*
   - In honor of her perpetual virginity, *Hail Mary…*
   - In thanksgiving for her marriage to St. Joseph, *Hail Mary…*
   - In honor of her divine motherhood, *Hail Mary…*
   - In honor of her relationship with the three persons of the Trinity, *Hail Mary…*
   - In contemplation of her escape from the decay of death, *Hail Mary…*
   - In honor of her assumption to Heaven, *Hail Mary…*

- In honor of her esteemed place in Heaven, *Hail Mary...*

5. The Crowing of Mary
   - In contemplation of Heaven's rejoicing at her coronation, *Hail Mary...*
   - To acknowledge Mary as the Queen of Heaven and earth, *Hail Mary...*
   - To honor Mary as Queen of angels and men, *Hail Mary...*
   - In contemplation of Mary as the treasury of grace, *Hail Mary...*
   - In honor of Mary as the destroyer of the devil, *Hail Mary...*
   - In honor of Mary as the safe refuge of sinners, *Hail Mary...*
   - In honor of Mary as the nurturing mother of sinner, *Hail Mary...*
   - In contemplation of Mary as the joy and delight of the just, *Hail Mary...*
   - In contemplation of Mary as the powerful relief for the afflicted, *Hail Mary...*
   - To ask that Mary become the Queen of our hearts, *Hail Mary...*

More on Marian Devotion:

Loving Mary Changes Everything

As soon as we start talking about the role of Mary in our spiritual lives, alarm bells begin to sound in many people's minds. If you're Catholic and you have never been accused of worshipping Mary, then buckle up, because it's coming! There are many fears about loving and honoring Mary too much, and the intention behind this is usually based on a good thing. Of course, we *all* want to be sure that God remains first in our lives. Ironically, and yet naturally, this is the goal of the Blessed Mother as well.

Mary can't and won't ever do anything that points in any direction other than Jesus. Venerable Fulton Sheen gives us a great analogy. He says that Mary is like the moon, which radiates beauty and light. The moon however has no light of its own; it is only a reflection of the sun. This is true for the Blessed Mother as well. She radiates the light of the Lord and reflects that light into the darkness. He is the only reason for her beauty and when we look at her we are really seeing his handiwork!

Take, for example, an artist who is debuting his greatest masterpiece at a famous museum. As people come to view his work and comment on its many qualities, magnificence and intricacies, the artist wouldn't be offended. You would not find him standing nearby annoyed as he proclaimed, "What about me?! Aren't I beautiful?" Of course, when the painting is admired the artist gets all the glory. The painting is only praised because of the talent of the artist.

Saint Teresa of Calcutta also illustrates that we have nothing to fear when it comes to loving Mary too much. As she was preparing to give a talk at a Theological conference, she heard that several theologians were arguing about this very topic. Some thought that we could surely love Mary too much; others thought she wasn't loved enough. In response, Mother Teresa decided to settle the issue. She dauntlessly approached the podium and addressed the crowd. The auditorium waited in anticipation to hear what this short-statured, spiritual giant had to say. Mother settled in the issue in just six words: "Love Mary as Jesus loved her." If there was ever a moment for a mic-drop— this was it.

You see, we can never love Mary as much as Jesus does! In fact, he had so much confidence in her that he put his very life into her hands. The truth is that human babies are more dependent on their parents than any other creature. Years before becoming parents, we realized this fact one evening while watching a nature special about the Great Migration. The documentary was set in Africa and followed a herd of wildebeests throughout the Serengeti. At the completion of the Great Migration, the wildebeests gave birth to their babies out in the wild. The narrator explained that the wildebeest babies must be able to stand almost immediately after birth in order to survive. If a calf is unable to walk, it will become a liability to the survival of the herd and will have to be abandoned. As the voiceover explained this, the video panned to one of the calves desperately trying to stand. The camera backed away to reveal vultures and foxes eager to attack the calf if it didn't make it. As the soundtrack grew increasingly mournful, I grew increasingly anxious!

The mother wildebeest continued to coax him to get up but this little guy's skinny stick-like legs just keep collapsing over and over again! Suddenly I found myself at the edge of my couch cushion begging, "STAND, WILDEBEEST, STAND!" Finally, he got up! The music turned celebratory and the mother wildebeest showed her pride and excitement in wildebeest fashion. The vultures were clearly disappointed but I was gasping, "Thank you Jesus!" Amazingly, wildebeests and other animals born in the wild have the minimal yet ever crucial survival skills immediately after birth.

As parents, we can attest that human babies are really the most pathetic animals in the world… and I mean that in a very sentimental way. We have three children of our own, and, practically speaking, they don't contribute much of anything to our household. They don't make any money, they destroy our house, and they eat all our food. A newborn baby takes seemingly years before it can take care of its own most basic needs. They rely 100% on their parents.

Almost inconceivably, this was the way that Jesus chose to come into the world. He could've come on clouds with chariots and thunder, but he chose to come through Mary. He elected to make himself wholly dependent on her until he could provide for himself. *The Lord wants us to go back to him in the very same way he came to us.* Jesus wants us to depend on her to show us the way.

This began in Jesus' first nine months as a human. During this time, the Body and Blood that we receive in the Eucharist was physically present within the Blessed Mother. As Catholics, we believe that the holiest place in the Church is the tabernacle, which is the place where the Eucharist is kept. Mary became a living, breathing tabernacle for her entire pregnancy!

Science has shown us recently how God desired to take this bond even further. The latest research has uncovered a phenomenon called *microchimerism.* Microchimerism proves that after pregnancy, a small number of cells from the child remain in the mother forever.[5] In a very real biological sense, mothers carry their child within them for life!. Mother Mary experienced this bond with the Lord spiritually, physically and literally for her entire life... and into eternity!

As if this wasn't enough, Jesus went on to live in Mary's house. By definition, this is equivalent to Mary's entire day spent in Eucharistic Adoration. Could we ask for a more suitable person than the first Christian to be our own mother to wrap us in her arms and form us in the faith? We know by definition that Jesus' physical heart was formed in Mary. He wants your heart to be formed in her as well.

Obviously, no one knows Jesus better than Mary. Mothers have a specific insight into their children. When our one-year old gets quiet, we know she is probably playing in the toilet. When she cries from the other room, we can tell if it's a hurt cry, a tantrum cry or a fake cry. Likewise, Mary could identify Jesus' cry (the voice of God!) above the noises of a crowded room. As he grew, his mother knew every mannerism, every food preference and how to tell that something was wrong just by the tone of his voice or subtle expression on his face.

More so, Mary heard her Son's message and ministry for thirty years before he began to speak publicly. Who better to introduce us to the Savior than the woman who taught him to walk

---

[5] http://www.microchimerism.org/

and picked him up when he fell? Who better than the one who was there when he was brought into the world and there when he died? Jesus adored his mother and he still does! No one loves Mary more than God, and we shouldn't be afraid to love or trust Mary... because we will never love her as much as Jesus!

This reality could only come to fruition through Mary's unfaltering faithfulness to God for all of her life. We can sometimes take for granted the magnitude of Mary's "yes" because we don't fully relate to the suffering God's people experienced as they waited for a Savior. We read the Old Testament in light of what we already know: the end of the story. In high school, my mom and I went through a phase where we would take turns reading murder mysteries. She would always begin by reading the last chapter first. Of course, this changed her experience of the whole story! Likewise, we read the Old Testament in context of the New. Let's try for a moment to relate to the anticipation of the Jewish people.

We know that from the time of the fall of Adam and Eve that the doors of Heaven were closed. God promised to send a Redeemer, but mankind would have to wait to be prepared and refined until "the fullness of time" (Gal 4:4-7 NAB). This was the reality for God's people. Imagine approaching your death and knowing you weren't going to Heaven. No one would. All souls would wait, some for thousands and thousands of years for their judgment. There was no Savior. Picture yourself growing older, losing family members and friends and knowing, they weren't going to "a better place." These souls would be imprisoned, awaiting the Messiah... and no one knew when he would be arriving. When we consider this, it becomes clear that we would be **starving** for a Savior.

Suddenly, the Lord allows the salvation of the world to hang on the response of a young, ordinary, teenage girl. In this moment, all of creation holds its breath and it awaits her reply: "Yes." She exclaims, "Be it done unto me according to your word" (Lk 1:38). In this moment, the flesh that is nailed to the Cross for our salvation is formed in her very womb. *It changes everything.*

Whoever you are, wherever you are in your relationship with the Blessed Mother, I am certain she wants to go deeper with you. Individually and as a couple, we would both cite Marian Consecration as a decisive turning point in our relationship with the Lord. This, "yes" that we gave to Jesus, through Mary, was returned through an exchange of hearts. This is why the "Champion of Mariology," St. Louis De Montefort, can say, "The more a soul is consecrated to Mary, the more it is consecrated to Jesus." The Blessed Mother promises that if you give her your heart, she will replace it with hers. We no longer love Jesus with our imperfect and sinful heart alone but we love him with Mary's Immaculate Heart. When Jesus receives our prayers, he receives them through her perfect heart.

Fatima and the Call to Consecration

Consecrating yourself for intimacy with Jesus through the intercession of Mary is a big step, and doing so as a teen is particularly special. The Lord has a knack for using young people, and the Scriptures cite his choices of adolescent prophets and heroes many times. Not only was Mary a teenager when she said "yes" at the Annunciation, but one of the most famous accounts of Marian Consecration begins with three very young individuals. Lucia, Jacinta and Francisco were the age of grade school children when Mary began visiting them in Fatima, Portugal in 1917. Mary explained that she had a message for all men, women and children living in this age. She described in fervor the corrupt nature of the world – from violent and bloody wars to the destructive ideologies and sins of impurity. The children heard of the heart of God and his desire for peace. During one of their many visits from the Blessed Mother, they were even shown a vision of hell. Later, Lucia described the horror and terror she experienced from this vision that lasted for only a moment. She said that the souls falling into hell, specifically from sins of impurity, were as thick as a snowfall. Remember that this was the age well before the sexual revolution, hook-up culture and invention of the internet. The Blessed Mother said,

"You saw hell where the souls of poor sinners go. In order to save them, God wishes to establish devotion to my Immaculate Heart in the world.

If people do what I ask, many souls will be saved and there will be peace."

So, what did Mary ask? The messages of Fatima are summed up in three words: prayer, reparation and consecration. She understood that these practices don't change God— they change us. When we center our lives on praying, repenting and devoting ourselves to a life like hers, everything changes. Of course, for the purposes of this book, we would especially like to emphasize this call to consecration. Mary specifically asked for the consecration of Russia to her Immaculate Heart. This was a prophetic message because, in the generations that followed, Russia rose in power spreading its communism ideologies and causing immense despair and religious persecution. Certainly, three small children would have had no understanding of such things. They weren't making this stuff up!

The children of Fatima had many skeptics, including their family and clergy. Yet, Mary's faithfulness to them inspired a continual faithfulness to her. Mary promised the children to appear on October 13th, 1917 with a "miracle that all might believe." 70,000 people gathered that day in a large muddy field waiting to discover if the claim of Mary's visitations were too good to be true. Suddenly, in the exact spot the children had predicted, the sun overhead began to move. Thousands of people cried out as the sun "danced" across the sky. The onlookers could look directly at the sun without damaging or hurting their eyes. It appeared to change colors and cast shades of light among the crowds. Some experienced joy and delight, while others feared for their lives. In a final swoop, the sun seemed to break free from the sky and come rushing toward the earth as many shrieked in horror expecting the end of the world. However, as the sun resumed its proper place in the sky, these eye-witnesses saw an image of the Holy Family above them. There was little doubt that these children were in fact telling the truth about the beautiful lady they had claimed to see.

Fast-forward 64 years exactly from the day of the first apparition, and we find Pope Saint John Paul II driving around St. Peter's Square, greeting the faithful who have come to Rome. Suddenly, shots ring out from the crowd and the Holy Father collapses. On this Feast of Our Lady of Fatima, the Pope was rushed to the hospital. He endured a five-hour surgery, only to find that the bullet missed his aorta by a few millimeters. Throughout the chaos and immense agony, the Pope found himself fixated on the Blessed Mother.

While recovering, the Pope asked for everything that was written on Our Lady of Fatima and her call for Marian Consecration. He was convinced that his miraculous survival was her doing. Famously, the Holy Father visited his would-be-assassin in a bleak prison cell to offer his heart-felt forgiveness. When he saw him, the shooter asked the Holy Father why he wasn't dead. This trained and skilled marksman, who had fired from close range, couldn't reconcile how his mission had failed. Without hesitation, JPII confirmed, "one hand fired the bullet, but a motherly hand guided its path."

In response to reading the documentation of Mary's request to the children at Fatima, the Pope was convicted that it was time to fulfill Our Lady's request to consecrate Russia. JPII decided that he would do so by offering not just Russia, but the entire world to Mary through an Act of Consecration. Exactly one year after the shooting, on May 13th 1982, Saint John Paul II traveled to Fatima to complete this Act of Consecration. As a personal offering of his gratitude, the Holy Father had the bullet from his assassination attempt soldered into the crown of the statue of Our Lady of Fatima. He renewed this consecration multiple times in the years that followed. As we know, true to Mary's prophesy, Russia did not spread its errors around the world. Less than a decade later, history books record the fall of Russia's Iron Curtain, and, therefore, the fulfillment of the promise of the Blessed Mother. Friends, this is the power of Marian Consecration.

Mary has promises for you as well. Through this Act of Consecration, the Blessed Mother desires to help you tear down the walls in your life that keep you from the freedom you desire. Mary taught the people of Fatima to pray. Throughout the next 33-days, she will pray for you and with you in this next step of devotion. Her motherly hand wants to guide your heart as well.

ABOUT THE AUTHORS

Mark and Katie Hartfiel are proud Texans who live with their children in Houston. Mark is the Vice President of Paradisus Dei, Inc. which the ministry responsible for family based programs such as, That Man is You!, The Choice Wine, and the Woman In Love Purity Retreat. He is also the author of *School of Nazareth*, a 30 day devotional for men based on the life of St. Joseph. Katie is a speaker and author of *Woman In Love* for young women. They can be found at paradisusdei.org and womaninlove.org.